Easy Review ™

CORPORATIONS

and other

BUSINESS ASSOCIATIONS

BY

Amy B. Gitlitz, *J.D.*
Cardozo School of Law

Contributing Editors

Allison B. Hoch, *J.D.*
Cardozo School of Law

Raymond A. Lombardo, *J.D.*
Fordham Law School

Randy J. Riley, *J.D.*
Seton Hall Law School

Consulting Editor

Mitchell D. Hollander, *Esq.*

Law Rules Publishing Corporation

(800)371-1271

Editorial Staff

Jared S. Kalina, *J.D.*
Cardozo School of Law

Daniel F. Kinsella

Blair P. Pieri

Copyright © 1997, 1998, By LAW RULES PUBLISHING CORPORATION
184 Central Avenue
Old Tappan, NJ 07675 - 2234
(800)371-1271

Library of Congress

ISBN 1-887426-44-2

Note: This review publication is not meant to replace required texts as a substitute or otherwise. This publication should not be quoted from or cited to. It is meant only to be used as a reminder of some subject matter and is not a substitute for a comprehensive understanding of the actual materials which it references or outlines .

TABLE OF CONTENTS

I.   AGENCY

A .   Agency Law:

Agency law governs the relationship between all the principals, agents, and any third party with whom the agent deals with on the principal's behest.

B.   Agent is:

1. Mutual Consent

    a. The principal must ***manifest an intent*** that the agent is acting on their behalf and the agent must accept that responsibility.

    b. This manifestation can be implied by conduct or words.

2. Acts on Another's Behalf

3. Must be under the authority of Another

    a. Restatement 2nd of Agency § 1.

    b. Agent acts according to the desires of the principal.

    c. Recommendations may be seen by the courts as mandatory acts to create an agency.

C. **Relationships which are not Agencies:**

1. Creditor/Debtor
   a. A debtor who imposes a requirement on a creditor to allow a loan. In this situation there is no agency relationship, unless:
      (1) Creditor has veto power over business acts; or
      (2) Creditor has control over salary, employment requirements, contracts, purchases, dividends, etc.
   b. A creditor who assumes ***de facto control*** over the business operations of a debtor may be liable for the acts of the debtor in connection with the business. In this situation, the court must consider the following:
      (1) Motivation for the assumption of control;
      (2) How the debtor and creditor represented themselves to the third party;
      (3) How much the creditor is involved in the day-to-day operations of the debtor.

2. Supplier/Buyer
   a. Supplier is:
      (1) A person who receives a ***fixed price*** for the property regardless of the price actually paid by him. This is the most important determination of a supplier.
      (2) A person who conducts business in his own name and receives title to any property in his own name.
      (3) A person who buying and/or selling similar property as an independent business.
   b. A supplier will be an agent if:
      (1) Acquires property from a third person;
      (2) Conveys it to another;
      (3) The benefit was primarily for the benefit of the other rather than for self.

D. Agency Creation

1. No consideration necessary.

2. Words.

3. Conduct.

4. Written or oral permissible.

5. Need mutual consent.

E. Types of Agents

1. General Agent
   a. Broad unlimited power to act.
   b. Continuity of service.
   c. Can act on several different transactions.

2. Specific Agent
   a. Limited powers.
   b. Narrow to certain usually one transaction.
   c. Usually time limitation (on this deal only).

F. Agent acts on behalf of the Principal

1. Restatement 2nd of Agency § 1.

2. *Disclosure* - a principal is disclosed if at the time of the transaction between the agent and the third party, the third party knows that the agent is acting on behalf of the principal.

3. ***Partially Disclosed*** - a principal is partially disclosed if at the time of the transaction the third party knows that the agent is acting on behalf of another but that other's identity is not known.

4. ***Undisclosed*** - a principal is undisclosed if at the time of transaction the third party believes that the agent is acting at his own behest.

G. Liability of Principal to Third Party for Acts of Agent

1. Actual Authority

    a. If the principal's words or conduct would lead a *reasonable person to believe that the Agent* had the authority to act in such a manner.

    b. *Implied* - power is inferred from the words used by the principal or from the nature or customs in the business. ("Do whatever is necessary.")

    c. *Express* - power that is specifically used to tell agent what to do. ("I want you to illegally tap his phone to see hear his bidding plans.")

    d. *Incidental* - powers of authority used to assist in carrying out main goal. ("I want you to sell my painting to John who lives in Hawaii." The person has the incidental authority to book plane tickets to Hawaii in the principal's name).

2. Apparent Authority

    a. If the words or conduct of the principal would have caused a reasonable person in the *third parties position to believe* that the principal had authorized the agent to act on their behalf.

    b. Principal appoints agent to a position which carries with it recognized duties. The Treasurer of a company is the financial agent of the company and his acts if reasonable carry the apparent authority to act on money on behalf of the company.

    c. Principal authorizes agent to act but imposes a limitation not to be expected by the third party. ("Go buy food but not from Giant Supermarket." Agent purchases from Giant on the company credit. Principal is still liable to Giant for payment.)

3. Estoppel

    a. Principal is bound by words or actions and is estopped from changing his mind on the agency.

    b. For example, in one court case concerning a transaction the principal admits an agency relationship. In a subsequent case relating to the same transaction, the principal tries to show that there was no relationship. Principal is estopped from denying agency in second case.

4. Inherent Authority

    a. Authority to act if reasonable person in the principal's *position should have foreseen* the agent would be likely to take even though the action would be in violation of the Agent's instructions.

    b. The principal is responsible for the neglect or disobedient acts of the agent if they are foreseeable.

    c. Includes:

        (1) The power to subject the principal to liability in tort based on actions within the scope of employment; and

        (2) The power of a general agent to subject principal to liability based on contracts.

    d. A disclosed or partially disclosed principal is liable for an act done on his behalf by a general agent, even if the principal had expressly or impliedly forbidden the agent to act in this manner if:

        (1) The act is incidental to the transaction that the agent is authorized to conduct; and

        (2) The third party reasonably believes that the agent is authorized to act in such a manner.

    e. An undisclosed principal is liable for his agent's authorized activities, even though the agent does not disclosed the agency, when the third party believes the agent is acting on his own behalf. The rationale is:

        (1) The principal stood to benefit;

        (2) The principal allowed the ruse;

        (3) The agent would be liable to the third party and could sue the principal for indemnification.

    f. An undisclosed principal is also liable for most acts of his general agent even though the agent had neither actual nor apparent authority.

5. Emergency situations - The principal is liable for an agent's actions taken in an emergency situation in which the agent acts to benefit the principal.

6. Ratification of Action

    a. Even if the agent did not have actual, apparent, or inherent authority, the principal will be liable if the agent purported to act on the principal's behalf and the principal with knowledge of the material facts either:

        (1) Knowingly

            • affirmed the agent's conduct by manifesting an intention to treat the agent's conduct as authorized (express ratification); or

- engaged in conduct that was justifiable only if he a had such an intention (implied ratification).

(2) Objectively manifested:
- before the third party has withdrawn.
- the agreement was otherwise terminated.
- or the situation has so materially changed that it would be inequitable to hold the third party liable.

(3) Distinguish from acquiescence
- Agent performs a series of acts of a similar nature and the failure of the principal to object to them is an indication that the principal consents to the performance of the similar acts in the future under similar conditions (apparent authority).

H. Third Party's Liability to the Principal

If the principal could be liable under the contract then the third party is also liable under the contract.

I. Agent's Liability to the Third Party

1. If the principal was *undisclosed*, the *agent is fully liable* to the third party. Under a majority of courts, *however*, if the third party receives a judgment against one the other is automatically released from liability to the third party. However, the principal and agent can seek indemnification from the other.

2. If the principal was *partially disclosed*, the *agent is fully liable* to the third party.

3. If the principal was *disclosed*:
   a. and the principal is bound by the agent's actions (actual, apparent, inherent, or ratification), the agent is not liable to the third party.
   b. and the principal is not bound, the agent may be liable (implied warranty of authority – gap fillers of UCC).

J. Liability Agent and Principal

1. If agent breaches actual authority, principal can get indemnity from agent.

2. If agent incur reasonable expenses in pursuit of goal then principal must reimburse agent for those expenses.

K. Termination

1. Either party can terminate the relationship, even if a contract provision forbids it, through any unilateral action unless the agency is coupled with an interest. Either:
   a. Secure performance of duty.
   b. Protect title to property interest (i.e., creditor appoints bank to hold property as escrow).

2. Passage of time can terminate agency.

L. Agent's Duty of Loyalty

1. Agents must act:
   a. Reasonably; and
   b. In Good Faith.

2. Restatement 2nd of Agency § 387. Unless otherwise agreed, the agent has a duty to act for the sole benefit of the principal in all matters relating to the agency:
   a. Duty not to use confidential information gained in course of agency to the disadvantage of the principal;
   b. Duty to give all profits to principal in connection with the transaction. § 388 calls for *profits gained by*:
      (1) *Using or conveying to another confidential information* that leads to agent or other's profit. (Agent tells mom and dad to buy land because the principal is ready to start buying land in that area).
      (2) *A third party forfeiture* of commissions or down payment or security bond in repudiation of a contract.
      (3) *Any monies recovered* in violation of duty to principal even if principal has successfully sought payment from the third party. This is to encourage the agent fiduciary responsibility to the principal regardless of any outside recovered loss.
      (4) Exception: an agent can properly retain gratuities received on the account of the principal's business if an agreement to this effect is found and the donor's interests are not adverse to the principal.
   c. Duty not to deal with the principal as an adverse party in any other transaction without the principal's knowledge and consent. § 389.
   d. *Duty to deal fairly* with the principal and *to disclose all facts known* to the agent which the agent should reasonably know that would affect the principal's judgment in this matter, unless the principal expressly manifests that he does not want to know them.

II.   BUSINESS ASSOCIATIONS

A .   Business Forms

Tax treatment for each form of business is often a decisive factor in form choice.

1.   Sole Proprietorship (SP)
- Capital outlay is small;
- Personally liable for all debts;
- Difficult to raise capital, transfer, or sell;
- Based largely on human capital; and
- Tax individual on income.

2.   Joint Venture
- Business undertaking by two or more parties;
- Profits, losses and control are shared;
- Usually more limited in scope and duration than a partnership.

3.   Partnership

a.   General Partnership (GP)
Governed by a Partnership Agreement;
Each partner has unlimited individual liability for the debts of the partnership;
Evenly split between partners:
- Equal authority;
- Each is an agent for the partnership;
- Each partner is jointly and severally liable; and

Partnership files the tax return but partners are all taxed individually (Pass-Through Entity or Flow-Through Entity)

b. **Limited Partnership (LP)**

At least one general partner and one limited partner;

General partner is an active partner.

Limited partner acts more like an investor with little or no input in day to day business decisions.

Governed by statute (such as the Uniform Limited Partnership Act);

Created by filing a document with a state;

Requires a written agreement among the partners

Liability:

- General partner is fully liable;
- Limited partner is liable to the extent of investment.

General partner has full authority to bind the LP.

Limited partners may freely transfer their interest unless the partnership agreement provides otherwise. However, a general partner cannot transfer their interest unless <u>all</u> of the other general and limited partners agree.

- Generally, treated as a partnership for tax purposes.
- If structured as a corporation, then Limited Partnership looses its Flow-Through tax treatment.
- IRS uses the following four criteria to distinguish a partnership from a corporation:
  1. Continuity;
  2. Central management
  3. Limited liability; and
  4. Transferability of interest.

4. **Limited Liability Companies (LLC)**
   Hybrid of partnership and corporation:
   1. Limited liability of all members; and
   2. Generally taxed as a partnership.

5. **Corporation** - A corporation is a legal entity distinct from its shareholders.
   Note: A corporate shareholder normally has no personal liability for corporate liability, other than the investment. However, under circumstances more fully described *infra* the corporate veil can be pierced and then the shareholder will be held liable for corporate obligation and debt.

   Corporation sells shares.
   Authority structure:
   - Shareholder (SH) - is the owner, elects the Board of Directors and votes on major decisions.
   - Board of Directors (BOD) - Supervisor of the corporation and its business direction.
   - Officer - appointed by BOD and oversees corporations day-to-day operations.
   - Can have more than 35 shareholders.
   - Taxed at corporate level; profits to shareholder is taxed again as individual level (taxed 2X).

   C Corporation is a corporation subject to federal income tax at the corporate level.

6. **Closely Held Corporation or Close Corporation**
   Definition: Less than 30 stockholders; No Initial Public Offerings (IPO).
   Formation: Its formation is indicated in its charter.
   Shareholder Agreement Restricting Board Discretion:
   The majority of close corporation shareholders may remove power from directors and transfer it to themselves.

13

Management by Stockholders
>>100% of close corporation shareholders may agree to manage instead of directors, but the majority may end shareholder management; the charter contains a provision regarding:
>>• management by shareholders;
>>• shareholders subject to liabilities of directors.

Stockholder Option to dissolve the Corporation
>>Charter can provide for stockholders to dissolve.

7. **S Corporation** (same requirements as a closely held corporation or close corporation). However, note the following:
    *   Only domestic corporations qualify;
    *   Subchapter S *election* must be approved by the Internal Revenue Service (IRS introducing "check the box" treatment for Sub S election);
    *   Follows corporate structure and operation.
        Differs from corporation in that profit and loss from corporate operation flows through to the shareholder avoiding double taxation. Pass-through entity.
        Must have less than 35 distinct shareholders (individuals, estates or qualified trusts).

    Termination of Subchapter S Corporation occurs if:
    1) Over any 3 year period, more than 25% of corporation's gross receipts constitutes passive investment income.
    2) Number of shareholders exceed 35.
    3) More than one type of stock is issued.

    Once terminated, an S corporation cannot be recreated before the fifth taxable year beginning after the first year for which the termination or revocation was effective.

14

	CORPORATION	PARTNERSHIP GP= General Partnership LP= Limited Partnership	LIMITED LIABILITY COMPANY (LLC)
DEFINITION	•Legal entity made up of management and Board; Centralized management and Board of Directors. Separate entity from its shareholders (owners).	•Association of 2 or more as co-owners. •GP: All have equal voice. •LP: GPs have voice & LPs have no voice.	• Either member-managed or have separate management.
FORMATION	•Statutory mechanics (filing). •RMBCA 2.02 DGCL 102	•GP: Contractual/ Consent; •LP: Filing	File a certificate with the state.

	CORPORATION	PARTNERSHIP GP = General Partner LP = Limited Partner	LIMITED LIABILITY COMPANY (LLC)
LIABILITY	• Corporation is responsible for its own debt •Shareholders: Limited to the extent of their investment. •Corporation: Entity of itself & shareholders not exposed beyond investment. •(Shareholder can also serve as officers & enjoy limited liability.)	•GP: Unlimited liability. • LP: Limited liability for LPs & unlimited for GPs. (LP is similar to a shareholder in a corporation but can't actively participate in affairs or become a GP.)	
	•BOD and Officers make all decisions; Shareholder allowed to vote on fundamental changes. in corporation only; •Shareholders elect and remove board members, but can't act on behalf of the corporation or participate in the daily management.	GP: Each GP has a voice - and the GP's make all decisions. •Each GP has the ability to bind the partnership. •LP: No voice in management. However, there is no bright line, definition for "Active Management."	•Operating agreement provides who shall manage. •If no agreement, VOICE = share of contribution.

	CORPORATION	PARTNERSHIP GP = General Partner LP = Limited Partner	LIMITED LIABILITY COMPANY (LLC)
FINANCING	•Issue stock; •Loans; •Sell equity securities (bonds, notes)	•GP: Obtain new partners, loans, injections from existing partners. •LP: Same as GP.	•Sell membership interests.
TRANSFER-ABILITY OF INTERESTS	•Shares can be easily sold without limitations. •Shares are easily transferable.	•GP: Need consent of all partners or transferable if authorized by partnership agreement. LP: Freely assignable, but may only exercise rights of LPs with consent of all remaining partners.	•Many statutes allow free assignment; others need consent of all members. HOWEVER, may not participate in management without consent of all members.
TAX	•DOUBLE TAX Corporation is taxed on its income and each shareholders must pay tax on what they receive in dividends.	•Profits FLOW THROUGH; partnership files an informational tax return only. Partners must individually file the income, deductions and credits on a pro rata basis. Not seen as an entity that is taxable under federal tax law.	•Not subject to corporate tax. No double taxation; flow through approach based on partnership model. However, like a partnership, LLC must avoid two of the following four criteria (1) continuity, (2)central management, (3)limited liability, and (4) transferability of interests. IRS Revenue Ruling 88-76.

17

III   CORPORATIONS

A.   Basic Terms

1.   **Corporate Statutes** (applicable to this outline)
   - Revised Model Business Corporation Act (RMBCA).
   - Delaware General Corporation Law (DGCL).
   - Note that each state has its own statutory scheme.

2.   **Organic Documents**
   - **Articles of Incorporation** (also known as charter or certificate of incorporation) - Constitution of the corporation.
   - **By-laws** - set forth details of internal governance of corporation.

3.   **Corporate Actors**
   - **Stockholders/Shareholders** - considered owners of the corporation.
   - **Board of Directors** - responsible for managing or supervising the corporation's business.
       Outside Directors are not corporate employees.
       Inside Directors are those who also serve as employees of the corporation (usually as an officer and a director).
   - **Officers** - manage the corporation on a daily basis. President, Vice President, Secretary and Treasurer.

4.   **Corporate Securities**
   a.   **Common Stock** - residual interest in the corporation after all senior claimants have been paid. Holders of common stock have voting rights and are entitled to distributions. Common stock may be divided into different classes.

b. **Preferred Stock** - ownership interest which may contain certain priorities, with respect to dividend, liquidation and distribution rights, over common stock. Preferred stock may be divided into different classes of preferred stockholders.

c. **Authorized Stock** is the maximum number of shares authorized for issuance issued without having to amend the Articles of Incorporation.

d. **Authorized but Unissued Stock**: is shares that were corporation and are held in its treasury (also known as **Treasury Stock**). This stock can be sold by the corporation on whatever terms its Board of Directors decides are reasonable.

e. **Outstanding Stock** are the shares of authorized shares of stock that have been issued and remain in the hands of the shareholder.

f. **Equity Securities** are common and preferred stock, the shareholder is at end of the line when it comes to distributions of corporate funds.

g. **Debt Securities** (i.e., bonds, debentures, notes) evidence obligations of the corporation and hold a priority over claims represented by equity security.

B.   Creating a Corporation

   1.   The incorporation process

      a.   The Articles of Incorporation

Corporation is a creature of state law;

To form a corporation the following three steps are crucial:

1) <u>Preparing</u> the Articles of Incorporation;
2) <u>Signing</u> the Articles by at least one incorporator; and
3) <u>Filing</u> the signed Articles at the state's Secretary of State (the commencement of the corporations existence).

      b. *Preparing* the Articles of Incorporation

The Articles of Incorporation <u>MUST</u> set forth:

1) Name of Corporation;
2) Number of Shares authorized for each class of stock issued;
3) Address of Corporation;
4) Name and Address of Incorporators; and
5) Name of the Agent; and
6) Nature of the business to be conducted.

The Articles of Incorporation <u>MAY</u> set forth:

1) Name and Address of directors;
2) Provisions regarding:
   - Corporations purpose;
   - Regulating affairs;
   - Powers of Corporation;
   - Par value (Stated Value) of shares;
   - Imposition of personal liability of shareholders.
3) Any By-laws;
4) Limitations on reliving director's personal liability.

RMBCA	DGCL
§2.02 - Articles of Incorporation •<u>Must</u> contain: corporation's name (see 4.01); number of shares authorized to issue; street address of corporation's initial registered office and name of its initial registered agent; and name and address of incorporator(s). •<u>May</u> contain: purpose of corporation; par value; duration, unless perpetual name & addresses of initial directors; powers of the board, officers & shareholders; personal liability provision.	**§102 - Contents of Certificate of Incorporation** •<u>Must</u> contain: name; address & name of registered agent; purpose of business; number of shares of authorized stock; par value; name and address of Incorporator(s); whether the Incorporator's powers will terminate upon filing and name & address of initial directors. •<u>May</u> contain: limiting purpose of corporation; preemptive rights; vote of a larger portion of the stock; limiting duration of corporation's existence; personal liability limitation. Note: The name of the corporation shall not contain the work "Bank" or any variation thereof.
§2.03 - Incorporation •File with the secretary of state. The Corporations existence begins at filing.	**§103 - Execution, Acknowledgment, Filing, Recording and Effective Date of Original Cert. of Incorp. and Other Instruments** •File a certificate of incorporation signed by the incorporator(s) with Secretary of State. the Certificate is effective upon filing date (unless otherwise noted). Existence begins with filing (§ 106).

RMBCA	DGCL
§2.05 - Organization of Corporation •Initial organizational meeting of Board or Incorporators to elect directors and complete the organization of the corporation. •Any action to be taken can be taken without meeting if each sign the instrument saying so. •Meeting may be held in or out of state.	**§108 - Organization Meeting of Incorporators or Directors named in Certificate of Incorporation** •Organizational meeting of board or Incorporators to adopt by-laws and elect directors; •At least 2 day written notice of the meeting (time, place & purpose) is required. •Any action to be taken can be taken without meeting if each sign instrument saying so.
§2.06 - By-laws •Initially adopted by the Board or Incorporators. •Contains provisions regulating and managing the business.	**§109 - By-laws** Initially adopted by the Board or the Incorporators; once payment is made for stock, only the shareholders have the power to adopt, amend or repeal the By-laws (unless the articles of incorporation states otherwise). •May contain any provision regulating and managing the business.

RMBCA	DGCL
§3.01 - Purposes of corporation •Engaging in any lawful business unless limited purpose set out in the Articles of Incorporation. **§3.01 - General Powers** •Corporation has perpetual existence the right to sue, and use of corporate seal.	**•§101 - Purposes of Corporation** •A corporation may be incorporated to conduct or promote any lawful business or purpose, except as otherwise provided in constitution or the law of Delaware.
§8.01 Requirement for & Duties of the Board •All corporate powers and business management is under the board. **§8.02 Qualification of Directors** •Prescribed by the articles of incorporation. •No need to be a shareholder or a resident of the state of incorporation. **§8.03 - Number and Election of Directors** •Fix the number of directors in the of Articles of Incorporation or By-laws; •If Board is allowed to change its number, up to 30%, any greater change must be approved by shareholders. •May be a variable range for size of Board (i.e., 7-9 directors). •Board is elected at the annual meeting.	**§141- Board of Directors** • (a);All corporation management is under the Board; • (b) One or more members as by-laws dictate; directors need not be shareholders; the certificate of incorporation will list more numbers and the qualifications; • (c) Can have committees; • (d) Directors (Staggered Board) may be divided into up to 3 classes; •No need to have all directors present at the meeting if they consent in writing; •May hold meeting outside the state; • (h) Board can fix the director's compensation; • (I) Members of the board or committee may participate in board meetings through the telephone, as long as the directors can simultaneously hear each other; • (k)Any director or entire Board may be removed with or without cause.

RMBCA	DGCL
§8.11 Compensation of Directors •The board fixes the directors compensation unless the articles of incorporation states otherwise. •**§8.20 Meetings** Can have board meetings within or without the state. •Members of the board can participate through any method where all directors participating can simultaneously hear each other (i.e., telephone). **§8.25 Committees** Can create committees of two or more members.	
§10.03 - Amendment of Articles of Incorporation by Board and Shareholder •Board may propose amendments to Articles of Incorporation for submission to shareholders. •For amendment to be adopted, it must be approved by either majority of shareholders or the amounts stated in §7.25 & §7.26; and, Board must notify the shareholders of the meeting. **§10.20 - Amendment of By-laws by Board & Shareholder** * Board can amend the By-laws unless the charter says only the shareholders can; * Shareholders can repeal or amend even if the Board can also do so.	**§241 - Amendment of Certificate of Incorporation before receipt of payment for stock** Before payment for stock is received, the Certificate can be amended by a majority of the Incorporators. **§242 - Amendment of Certificate of Incorporation after receipt of payment for stock** Corporation may amend so as to: change name; change purpose; increase or decrease capital stock; affect the right of shareholders; make new classes of stock; and change period of duration. Amendments are made by the board adopting a resolution; then a majority of shareholders must approve (unless the articles of incorporation state otherwise).

c.   Where to incorporate

Delaware is the most hospitable state for large corporations:
- Simplified management.
- Well defined common and statutory law.
- Need legislative vote to change corporate charter.
- Substantial human capital - judges, etc.
- Expedited court procedures
    See e.g., Time v. Paramount
- Flexible corporate laws
    See e.g. § 141(b) supra
    See DGCL § 109(a) supra

Small corporations will only pick one state for incorporation and doing business. Otherwise, the corporation is subject to pay taxes in more than one state.

The *place of incorporation* determines your governing law, no matter where the corporation does business.
Consequently, states will try to sell their corporate statutes. There is a competition among states to attract those that incorporate.

Internal Affairs Doctrine

Delaware laws may not embody either a race to the top or the bottom, but might simply be quantitatively better in many respects. *See* DGCL § 109.
- **Race to the top** - Maximize shareholders' wealth.
- **Race to the bottom** - Maximize managers' interest.

Note: It is unfair to put the managers interest above the shareholders, but even if there is a race to the bottom, it can never go too far because of management's' fiduciary obligations including a restriction against self dealing for the managers. The courts will not allow it because it may constitute a breach of the **Duty of Loyalty**.

2. Liability for actions before incorporation

a. Promoter (Incorporator)---person who participates in the formation of the corporation.

Fiduciary Duties of Incorporation Include:

Arrange compliance with the legal and statutory requirements; Secure initial capitalization; and enter into necessary contracts. Incorporators have the power to do anything necessary to perfect the organization of the corporation. It is a purely mechanical job. They sign the articles and arrange for filing but have *no responsibilities after* incorporation unless they become directors or officers.

Rule: The corporation can be held liable on any contracts that the promoter (incorporator) enters into if the corporation ratifies or adopts the contract (either express or by implication). There usually needs to be some affirmative act of ratification such as:

- Accepting the benefits of the contract;
- Formal action by the board;
- Use of the materials or services obtained under the contract;
- The promoters are treated as directors (especially when the board is entirely composed of promoters).

See, e.g., D.A. McArthur v. Times Printing Co., 51 N.W. 216 (Minn. 1892); *Clifton v. Tomb*, 21 F. 2d 893 (4th Cir. 1947); *Chartrand v. Barney's Club, Inc.*, 380 F.2d 97 (9th Cir. 1967); *Jacobson v. Stern*, 605 P.2d 198 (Nev. 1980).

Note: The third party to any contract by the incorporator (promoter) is also bound by the contract.

3. Liability of Promoters (Incorporators)

Rule: Generally, if the corporation is never formed but the Promoter entered into contracts, the Promoter is personally liable for failure to act on the contract unless he has made it specifically clear that he is contracting solely on behalf of the proposed corporation.

- This is true even though the contract was intended to benefit the corporation.
- Very often courts will look at whether or not the contract requires service or performance *before formation.*
- Courts will also look at the intent of the parties.

RMBCA § 2.04	All persons purporting to act on behalf of the corporation knowing that it is not yet incorporated are jointly and severally liable for all acts.

Stanley J. How & Associates v. Boss, 222 F. Supp. 936 (S.D. Iowa 1963)
> **Held**: A promoter (incorporator) liable on a contract with an architect because the parties intended that the Promoters would pay if the corporation did not.

Quaker Hill v. Parr, 364 P.2d 1056 (Colo. 1961)
> **Held**: Promoter not liable because the supplier agreed to seek payment only from the corporation, not the promoters.

Company Stores Development. Corp. v. Pottery Warehouse, Inc., 733 S.W.2d 886 (Tenn. App. 1987)
> **Held**: Promoter is not personally liable when the supplier knew that the corporation was not yet in existence but failed to require the promoter to sign an agreement of personal liability.

4.   Defective Incorporation

a. *De jure Corporations* - Created when an incorporator complies substantially with the rules governing incorporation. If noncompliance is limited to unimportant matters then the *de jure* corporation is treated as a corporation that has complied with the incorporation process. A *de jure* corporation existence cannot be attacked by anyone including the state.

b. *De facto Corporation* - Is created when (1) there has been a good faith attempt to incorporate and (2) the corporation has engaged in business. A state can challenge the *de facto* corporations existence. As for third parties, a *de facto* corporation is treated as a *de jure* corporation.

The difference between a *de jure* and a *de facto* corporation is the degree of compliance within the incorporation process.

c. *Corporation by Estoppel* - A corporation by estoppel is created when there is no good faith attempt to incorporate. The corporation by estoppel existence may be attacked by anyone except third parties who have dealt with the entity as if it was a corporation.

What if They Never Incorporate?
- **Reasonable Expectations Rule** - If attorney leads an individual into thinking that she represents them, an attorney-client relationship exists.
   To avoid this, an attorney should state her fiduciary obligations; and ask the client what they expect.

5.   **The Role of the Attorney**

Entity Rule
- If an attorney represents an individual to form a corporation, the attorney represents the *corporation* not the *individual*.
- Therefore, there is no individual protection or attorney client privilege.
- *Retroactive* for pre-incorporation action with intent to incorporate.

The attorney must make full disclosure to all parties of whom her fiduciary obligations lie:
>   "I represent the corporation before anyone else."
>   "I still have an obligation with individuals for actions in past."

C. Amending the by-laws and Articles of Incorporation

- An *Organizational Meeting* is held to adopt the by-laws, elect directors (unless already named in the charter) and further act to perfect the organization of the corporation.
- Shareholders have some power with regard to amending or adopting the by-laws and articles of incorporation (unless the charter provides otherwise).

RMBCA	DGCL
§10.20 Amendment of the By-laws •The board may amend or repeal the by-laws unless: 1. The articles reserve this power exclusively to the shareholders; or 2. The shareholders in amending or repealing a particular by-law expressly provides that the board may not amend or repeal it. •The shareholders may also appeal or amend the by-laws.	**§109 (a) By-laws** •Once a corporation has received payment for stock, only the shareholders have the power to adopt, amend or repeal by-laws; •If the articles allow it, the directors may also have the power to amend or repeal but this will not divest or limit the shareholders' power to amend the By-laws.
10.21 By-law increasing Quorum or Voting Requirement for Shareholder •Shareholders may fix greater or lesser voting or quorum requirements in by-laws if the articles expressly allow it; •Any such change must meet the higher of the new or old quorum / voting requirements; •Once fixed, the board cannot change quorum or voting requirements.	

Note: DGCL § 109 is a good example of DE flexibility.

1. **The Articles of Incorporation:** is the instrument which is filed to create the corporation. It is sometimes called:
    *   Certificate of Incorporation;
    *   Articles of Association; or
    *   Charter.

2. **Procedure for Amendment of the Articles of Incorporation** :
    The Board of Directors propose the amendment to the shareholders and a majority of stockholders (some states require 2/3) must adopt the amendment. DGCL 242(b)

3. **By-laws:** Rules adopted for the governance of the corporation and its corporate matters. The power to make, amend or repeal the By-laws is in the hands of the stockholders, however, sometimes the Articles of Incorporation allow the board to do so.

    Fundamental changes in the corporation are established by amendment of the Articles of Incorporation or the By-laws.

D. Source of Corporate Powers

1. Express and Implied Powers

Corporate powers come from both the certificate of incorporation and the "general powers" provisions in the statutes. The statutes list powers that the corporation has whether or not the certificate of corporation grants them.

Note: Some statutes allow corporations to opt out of certain provisions through a by-law or certificate of incorporation provision.

- **Express Powers** are explicitly enumerated in the certificate of incorporation and the "general power" provisions of the statute.

- **Implied powers** are those powers that are reasonably necessary to accomplish the purposes laid out in the certificate of incorporation.

- **Corporate Purpose:**
  Corporations may have the same power as an individual to do all things necessary or convenient to carry out all of its business as long as it is a lawful act that will enable the corporation to carry out its business functions.

RMBCA	DGCL
§3.02 - Contains both general and specific powers •The corporation can do anything that an individual can do as long as it is necessary or convenient to carry out business including: •Sue or be sued; Have a corporate seal; Make and amend the by-laws; Purchase, lease & own real or personal property; Sell or otherwise convey property; Acquire, hold , vote & dispose of securities in other corporations; Make contracts; Borrow money; Issue securities; Mortgage property; Lend money; Conduct business within or without the state; Elect directors; Appoint officers; Fix compensation; Establish pension plans; Make donations. *The list of powers (above) is not limited.*	**§ 121 (general powers)** •The corporation can do anything under § 122 or any other law or charter as long as they are necessary and convenient to the business purpose. • **§ 122 (specific powers)** Perpetual existence; Have a Corporate Seal; Sue and be sued; acquire, hold & dispose of real and personal property; Appoint officers; Adopt & amend and repeal by-laws; conduct business within & and without the state; Establish pension plans; Acquire, hold, vote and dispose of securities in other corporations; provide insurance to directors, officers and employees; make contracts of guaranty and suretyship; lend money; Participate in partnerships, associations and other corporations with others any lawful business; wind up and dissolve itself. *This gives a little more power than the RMBCA.*

2. Ultra Vires

A claim that an act was beyond the power of the corporation (a corporation may not engage in activities outside the scope of the purposes for which the corporation was founded). However, current laws basically state that anything legal is within the power of the corporation.
Almost all states have explicitly abolished the doctrine of Ultra Vires as to lawsuits by or against third parties who have done business with the corporation.

a. **Statutes Removing the Problem of Ultra Vires**

RMBCA	DGCL
§ **3.01** - Every corporation has the purpose of engaging in any lawful business unless limited by the articles of incorporation § **3.04** - The validity of a corporate action may not be challenged on the ground that the corporation lacked the power to act unless it is through: A proceeding by a shareholder to enjoin the act. A proceeding by the corporation against an incumbent or former officer, director, employee or agent. A suit by the state Attorney General for judicial dissolution.	§ **102(a)(3)** - It is sufficient for the corporation to state that its purpose is to engage in any lawful act or activity for which the corporation may be organized under DGCL. § **124** - No Ultra Vires defense that the corporation lacked powers (same as RMBCA).

The Doctrine of Ultra Vires is no longer a problem. Neither the corporation nor any other person can claim that a contract is not enforceable because it violates the corporate purpose. However, even with this protection, the corporation *must not waste* its assets, etc. *See infra* Duty of Loyalty, Duty of Care discussions.

b. **Quo Warranto Action:** A common law writ used to test whether a corporation was validly organized or whether it has the power to engage in the business in which it is involved.

35

3.Corporate Power and social issues

RMBCA	DGCL
§3.02(13) - The corporation has the power to make charitable donations unless the charter or by-laws states otherwise. **§3.02(15)** - Charitable donations can be inconsistent with the business and affairs of the corporation; They must further the business purpose.	**§122(9)** - The corporation has the power to make donations for the public welfare or for charitable, scientific or educational purposes, and in time of war or other national emergency in aid thereof.

In general, any charitable gift by a corporation is tax deductible if it is not more than 10% of the corporation's income. This is considered a reasonable donation.

a. Constituency statutes:

- Corporations have been held to have the implied power to make reasonable charitable contributions, especially through *Constituency Statutes,* which allow the Board to take into account society at large. *See e.g.* PA Con Stat 1715 (Other Constituency Statutes). See Conrail/SCX/Northern Southern v.,.

- Nearly all states have now enacted statutory provisions explicitly allowing charitable contributions.

- **Reasonableness limitations** - Courts usually read such statutory language as authorizing only charitable donations that are *reasonable* in size, income and type. The corporation can easily make donations within the federal tax donations limitation of 10% of income. An excessive donation will be seen as waste and may be attacked as Ultra Vires primarily because of Director duties regarding shareholder and corporation property.

The problem is basic tension between the corporation's good (often = higher profits) v. community good (ex: keep the plant in the US).

Thus, because board members are dealing with others' property specifically shareholders, the board needs to put to use in way that protects and enhances that property.

- *Principle obligation is to the shareholders* - the Board's primary duty and fiduciary obligation is to the shareholders. A Director cannot act for the purpose of benefiting others. If a director has strong personal opinion regarding a matter, he should not vote.

- The Board must be able to make a *Solid Business Judgment*. Therefore, the Board cannot solely rely on ethical issues because:
    a) The Board cannot look to community and society concerns that conflict with fiduciary obligations.
    b) The Board *can't have merely incidental benefits to the shareholders.*

b.   Can the corporation act to further goals other than those related to profits?
--See, e.g., Dodge Brother v. Ford

Theodorah v. Henderson, 257 A. 2d 398 (Del. Ch. 1969)
The board disagreed on which charity the corporation should donate money to.

Rule: As long as a donation is reasonably limited with respect to amounts and purpose, A corporation can make a charitable contribution. However, a corporation must do so in accordance with its directors' *fiduciary obligations.*

- Corporations are allowed to make charitable contributions.
- Look at size of the gift in relation to the corporation's size.
- Here it was 10% of annual earnings, but this was acceptable.

Dodge v. Ford Motor Co., 170 N.W. 668 (Mich. 1919)
The case said Henry Ford could not run his corporation for social good, but rather for *profit to shareholders.* Must put interests of S/H's first ($).

Shlensky v. Wrigley, 237 N.E.2d 776 (Ill. App. Ct. 1968)
The court will not enter the situation only based on poor business judgment, there needs to be fraud, illegality, or a conflict of interest. Otherwise, the decision is up to the Board. Here, the fact that directors didn't want to put in lights was not in the best interest of the corporation. Because the property would become more valuable and would be best for the neighborhood.

c.   Purpose of Constituency Statutes:

1.   Move away from the idea of shareholder primacy.

2.   Authorize the Board to look at other interests -- state, economy, community, long-term, corporation's employees, suppliers, creditors, customers, etc.

3.   Could be good for the economy -- keeps businesses and jobs in the state.

4.   Delaware has not adopted a consistency statute, but DE does allow latitude. Look at Time Warner v. Paramount Case: allowed Time to turn

38

down Paramount's better offer b/c Board thought Time Warner better deal.

- Most large businesses are already incorporated in Delaware;
- Such a statute could prevent companies from developing there. Bad for the shareholders because this is not the only interest.

Note:

- Profit maximization is primary goal, but you can look to other things.
- Both the the RMBCA & DGCL put the power on the Board to make the decisions.
- Connecticut *requires* the corporation to consider constituency interests (others permit it, but do not require it).
- A risk of a corporate boycott is a great way to get the constituencies voice heard.

These statutes often move away from S/H primacy under the guise of allowing directors to promote "long term" interests. A way to allow directors to turn down lucrative buy outs that would dissolve or break up the corporation.

E.   Corporate Finance

1.   The corporations capital

a.   Tax considerations

1. A corporation can deduct interest payment on bonds (but recipient must pay tax).
2. A corporation can not deduct dividends or interest payments on dividends.
3. Corporations prefer debt, but this lowers the capital cushion and the IRS frowns on high debt and may treat it as ("thin" corporation debt) equity.

b.   Leverage risk allocation

If the interest rate is lower than the rate of return, the corporation will want to borrow to finance a deal. This will increase shareholders' risk; however, they will only do it if they are confident that leverage will work in their favor. If it goes the wrong way, it accelerates the downturn.

c.   Over indebtedness

If there is a significant debt to the shareholders, then the court will use the *Deep Rock Doctrine* to determine that shareholders' debt will be subordinated to the debt held by other creditors. Thus, the debt is treated like an equity in a bankruptcy proceeding.

2.   Sources of capital & liquidation and other preferences

Raising corporate capital brings into play three main interests: RISK, REWARD, & CONTROL.
Questions:
- Do the investors want profits? If yes, then issue stock.
- Do the investors want control? If yes, then issue stock.

- Do the investors want fixed payments? If yes, then debt is better or issue preferred stock.
- Do the investors want to avoid corporate taxes to the corporation? If yes, then interest payments are deductible by the corporation, therefore choose debt.
- Do the investors want priority in insolvency? If yes, then debt is preferred, rather than equity.

Sources of Corporate Financing:
1. Debt; and
2. Equity.

Financing Preferences

Debt   Preferred Stock   Common Stock

More liquid--*less liquid*

a. **Debt**

Debt Securities:
a) Bonds & debentures;
b) Liability of the corporation; not stockholders beyond their investment;
c) Corporation must pay interest on debt;
d) Can be redeemable or callable at a fixed price
e) or convertible into equity;
f) Holder has no control over the corporation
g) except by contract;
h) No voting power;
i) Rights entirely fixed through a contract;
j) Can be issued without shareholder approval;
k) Must be paid before dividends to shareholders;
l) Less risky than stocks; and
m) Interest is tax deductible to the corporation.

41

b. **Equity.** Equity Securities (must be paid for in cash or property or service - *not* a promissory note):
- Control of the corporation;
- Permanent commitment;
- Riskier, depends on profit.

Categories of Equity Securities:
- Authorized but not issued;
- Authorized and issued; or
- Authorized, issued and not outstanding (if the shares have been redeemed)(i.e., Treasury Stock).

1) **Authorized** means the number of shares authorized by the articles of incorporation to be issued (not the actual number of shares sold).

2) **Issued** means the authorized shares that have *actually been sold.* Thus, if the articles of incorporation authorize 100 shares and the corporation sells 50 in its initial public offering, only 50 issued shares.

3) **Outstanding -** authorized shares which have been issued and have *not* been repurchased or redeemed by the corporation. Thus, in the above example if the 50 shares have been sold by the corporation, they are issued and outstanding.

4) **Treasury Stock--** Shares that have been authorized and issued and then repurchased or redeemed. This stock is then held by the corporation (the corporation is essentially the shareholder of some of its own shares).

5) **Canceled Stock--** Once a share has been authorized and issued but the corporation repurchases it and no longer treats it as an outstanding share.

c.   **Classes of Shares**

RMBCA §§2.02 & 6.01(a) & DGCL §151 - Authorized Shares	
COMMON STOCK * Power to elect Board. * Right to distribution of assets. * <u>Voting rights</u>. * <u>Paid dividends</u>. * Distribution at liquidation. * Paid after debt and preferred stock. **RESIDUAL CLAIM.** * Rarely liquidated. * Greater right of participation and power. * Protected by the fiduciary obligation. * Can have many classes.	**PREFERRED STOCK** * Economic rights above the common shareholders; * Given a preferred payment. * Generally no voting rights (but they can). * May have *conversion rights* which allow them to convert to common stock upon occurrence of a specific event. * **3 types** sometimes can participate in the governance of the corporation but do not need to be; if they are, then they only receive payments when a distribution is made to common shareholders, AFTER payments to non-participating preferred shareholders; * **Cumulative** - unpaid dividends carry over into the following year and are paid before common; * **Non-cumulative** - unpaid dividends do not accumulate; * **Partially cumulative** - payment rolls over to the following year only if the prior year had sufficient earnings.

- A share of stock represents a stockholders interest in the corporation.
- Any person or group that acquires more than 15% of the corporations is an *"interested stockholder"*.

Cumulative preferred stock-- If dividend is not paid when due, the right to receive the dividend still accrues and all accumulated dividends accrued must be paid before any dividends are paid on common stock.

Redemption -- The corporation acquires some or all of a class of stock by paying a stipulated price to shareholders.
- •Shares acquired or "redeemed" are either canceled and thus are no longer outstanding or remain as treasury stock;
- •At least one class of shares must remain;
- •Shareholders may have the right to force the corporation to redeem the shares under certain circumstances. RMBCA § 6.01(c)(2) and DGCL § 151(b);
- •The corporation may reserve the right in the articles of incorporation to redeem shares at the discretion of the Board.

Repurchase - Shares are repurchased by the corporation.
Unlike redemption, this is not mandated by the Articles of Incorporation, it is governed by an agreement. Shares usually become part of the treasury stock, however under RMBCA § 6.31 since there is no treasury stock, the shares are automatically considered authorized but unissued.

Preemptive rights - A shareholder is entitled to purchase stocks when new shares are offered so that she can maintain her proportionate control without being diluted. Most public corporations opt not to have preemptive rights since shareholders can purchase shares through the open stock market.

Many private corporations allow preemptive rights since shareholders can not easily purchase shares.

RMBCA	DGCL
§6.30 - Shareholders' Preemptive Rights Corporation must elect to have preemptive rights.	Does not mention preemptive rights; However, §157 states that a corporation can authorize rights to purchase stock.

d. Legal capital

RMBCA	DGCL
§2.02(b)(iv) - Corporation <u>may</u> set forth Par value (enabling, not mandatory). If no par value is given, the corporation can issue stocks with any formula, minimum price, etc., if they have been redeemed. Thus, "No-Par value stocks" are allowed.	**§102(a)(4)** - Corporation must either set a Par value or state that there is no par value. Thus, it still uses the LEGAL capital system.
	§153 Consideration for Stock •Par value is a minimum value for stock. •If there is no par value then the board must determine the minimum price amount for the issuance of stock; •If no par value, then it is a price that the Board determines that will govern.
§6.21 & Official Comment - Issuance of Shares •Any tangible or intangible asset are valid consideration, as long as the Board acts with reasonable care and good faith including promissory notes and future services. • The value of non cash consideration must be adequate. •Decisions as to value is protected under the **"BJR."** •No par value, so no watered stock.	**§152 - Issuance of Stock; Lawful Consideration; Fully Paid Stock** •Board determines amount and nature of the consideration. •Cash, personal property, or services rendered are valid consideration -- promissory note and future service is not. •Still has par value, but it can be changed and you can have no par value stock.

e. **Consideration for stock**: *The Board determines the amount and nature of the consideration for stock (see supra* DGCL § 153).

Generally, stocks must be sold at least at par value. However in *Handley v. Stutz*, 139 U.S. 417 (1891) the Supreme Court held that a corporation whose capital is impaired can sell its stock at the best obtainable price even if it is below par value.
Par value is the face amount of a share of capital stock. Represents the minimum amount per share to be invested in the corporation when shares are originally issued.

a) **Watered Stock**--stock purchased at less than par value (not fully paid for).

b) **Discount (bonus) shares**--shares given at an amount much less than par value. This usually deals with shares given as compensation to an executive such as options.

c) **Over valued property or services**--If stock is watered a creditor may be able to recover from that stockholder if there is an intentional overvaluation of the price. (See DGCL §162; *Haneweld v. Bryan's Inc.*, 429 N.W.2d 414 (N.D. 1988).

d) **No Par Stock**-- (eliminates the problem of watered stock). Is stock that can be sold at whatever price the board determines is reasonable. However, the board must state the value of the consideration for the shares and the consideration paid (even if it is in property) must be legitimately worth that amount. (*See* DGCL 162).

e) **Paid-in-Surplus** - The amount paid for stock in excess of its par value.

f) **Subscription Rights (stock rights)**: The *contractual rights* of an existing shareholder to purchase additional shares of (the same kind) of stock when and if new shares are issued by the corporation.

46

g) **Repurchase Rights:** The contractual rights of a corporation to repurchase its own stock from shareholders. Often upon the occurrence of a certain event such as a specific stock price.

h) **Restriction of Transfer of Securities**: Restrictions allowed if *noted conspicuously* in the stock certificate and notice is given to the purchaser. Very often occurs in private corporations.

RMBCA	DGCL
Shareholder is not liable for the debts of the corporation **§6.22 - Liability of shareholders** •Only required to pay the consideration that is owed for the purchase of the stock. • Shareholders are personally liable for the debts of the corporation beyond what they owe for consideration unless the shareholder does an act making it liable.	Shareholder will be liable for failure to pay for stock in full **§162 - Liability of Stockholder or Subscriber for Stock Not Paid in Full** •If the entire consideration payable is not paid in full, then the shareholder is liable for creditors claims to the extent of the unpaid balance. **§156 - Partly Paid Shares** •Allows for partly paid issued shares that are callable. **§163 - Payment for Stock Not Paid in Full** •The capital stock must be paid in full by the shareholders at the request of the directors.

3. **Discussion of income statement and balance sheet accounting:**

a. The **income statement** is a report used to evaluate the performance of a business by matching its revenue and related expenses for a particular accounting period. Shows the net income or loss. Net income is the excess of revenue earned over the related expenses for a given period (the operating results). The alternative titles for the income statement include *earnings statement, statement of operations, and profit and loss statement.* The income statement is usually prepared and submitted with a balance sheet discussed *infra.*

Example of an income statement:

BLUE REALTY COMPANY
Income Statement
For the month ended July 31, 19--

Sales, commissions earned		$5,640
Expenses:		
Advertising expense	$ 630	
Office salaries expense	2,100	
Telephone expense	144	
Depreciation expense: building	150	
Depreciation expense: office equipment	45	
Total Expenses		3,069
Net Income		$2,571

The income statement measures the corporate earnings.
Corporate Earnings - funds generated by the business when the revenue earned exceeds the expenses incurred in obtaining that income:
    1) Can be used by the corporation to fund new business ventures.
    2) Can be used for dividend distribution.

48

b.   Balance sheet accounting:
The corporations assets and liabilities, debt and equity are portrayed
on the balance sheet. How assets are accounted (book or actual)
must be understood for a fair valuation of the corporations financial
position. Balance sheet accounting - will determine whether a
corporation can make a dividend distribution depending on the legal
test used.

Every business prepares a balance sheet at the end of the year, and
most companies prepare one at the end of each month to show the
financial position of the business at the end of a period.

A balance sheet consists of a listing of the assets and liabilities of a
business and the stockholders equity (for a corporation).

(i) **Assets** are economic resources which are owned by a
business and are expected to benefit future operations. Assets
may be in the form of buildings, machinery, merchandise,
valuable legal claims or rights; examples are amounts due
from customers, investments and intellectual property rights.
Assets are portrayed on the balance by their value:

Valuation of assets can be made at the cost or market
principle:
Cost basis provides for a <u>definite valuation</u> for it is simply
the dollars that have been invested in these resources.

Market values are constantly changing and estimates of
what prices assets could be sold for or are worth are largely
a matter of personal opinion.

Note: *Plant assets* are <u>usually shown</u> on the balance sheet at
current book value.
Book value of a *plant asset* is its cost minus the related
accumulated depreciation.

Rules for the valuation of assets varies:
NY, for ex, allows valuation of assets <u>at market</u> not original
cost. *See Randall v. Bailey* 23 NYS2d. 173 NYBCL §510.
DE uses <u>book value</u> **or** <u>market</u>: *see Morris v. Standard Gas and
Electric 63 A2d. 577 (1949).*

(ii) Liabilities are debts. Liabilities are portrayed on the balance
sheet as:
> **Accounts payable** are liabilities arising from purchase
> of merchandise and supplies on credit.
>
> **Note payable** is a formal written promise to pay a
> certain amount of money, plus interest, at a definite future
> time
>
> **Income tax payable** appears on the balance sheet as a
> form of liability only for the corporation because a
> corporation is a taxable entity.

(iii) Stockholders' equity is portrayed on the balance sheet as:
> **Capital stock** represents the amount invested in the
> business by its owners. Transferable units of ownership.
>
> **(iv) Retained earnings** represents the portion of
> stockholders equity which has been accumulated through
> profitable operation of the business. The corporation can
> choose to retain all or a portion of the corporate earnings in
> the business rather than distribute these earnings to
> stockholders as dividends.
>
> **Note**: The term retained earnings describes only the earnings
> which were **not** paid out in the form of dividends.
> Retained earnings *paid* would not appear on the balance
> sheet.

Example: The Balance Sheet

The Auto Wash
Balance Sheet
December 31, 19--

Assets		Liabilities & Stockholders' Equity		
Cash	$ 9,600	**Liabilities**:		
Notes receivable	10,000	Notes payable	$ 29,000	
Accounts receivable	800	Accounts payable	2,000	
Supplies	3,000	Income taxes payable	3,000	
Land	30,000	Total liabilities	$34,000	
Buildings	60,000	**Stockholders' equity**:		
Machinery & equipment	85,000	Capital stock	$65,000	
		Retained earnings	99,400	164,400
	$198,400			$198,400

Paid-in capital is the amounts invested in the corporation by its
 stockholders.

Stated capital is that portion of capital invested by stockholders which
 cannot be withdrawn. Also called **Legal capital** (See statutes
 supra page 45).

51

F.   Dividends: When can the corporation pay the shareholder a
dividend?

> **Dividend** - is a payment to the shareholders *out of the*
> *corporations earnings* of cash, property, or additional shares. (Note:
> Additional shares are not really a dividend, they divide ownership
> of the corporation by a greater number of shares.)

- The decision to pay out a dividend is generally protected by the
  Business Judgment Rule since they are made at the directors'
  discretion. The shareholders have no right to dividends--even if
  there are sufficient funds available, or if the corporation has a
  high earnings year. (*See, e.g. Gottfried v. Gottfried*, 73
  N.Y.S.2d 692 (1947)).

- Courts will rarely interfere with the directors' decisions to make
  a distribution because it is discretionary matter. However, if the
  shareholder's can prove that the directors acted in bad faith their
  discretion in refusing to declare a dividend a court might compel
  a dividend distribution.

> ***Dodge v. Ford Motor Co.***, 170 N.W. 668 (Mich. 1919)
>> The court interfered with the director's decision not to
>> declare a dividend in a year where the company had very
>> high earnings and cash flow.
>> **Rule:** A court will not uphold irrational decisions about
>> dividends that it determines to be an abuse of the director's
>> discretion.

Note:
- Courts are more likely to interfere with a decision in a close
  corporation because it is harder to sell the stock; therefore
  without dividends the owners may receive no benefit. (*See, e.g.*
  Smith v. Atlantic Properties, 422 N.E.2d 798 (Mass. 1981).
  where the court held that the fiduciary duty owed by the
  shareholder's in a close corporation may affect the power to
  declare a dividend).

- In a public corporation, the court is more likely to uphold the board's decision regarding dividends because the stocks can easily be sold on the open market.
- Once a dividend is declared, the shareholders become creditors of the corporation for the dividend amount - only if it is a cash dividend.
- *Conflict of interest* is a *tension* between the *shareholders and the creditors* when distributions are made to shareholders because the creditors want to ensure that no shareholders are paid before they are.

Many statutes hold that dividends can only be paid out if the corporation has a *Surplus in Net Assets* over its stated capital. (See, e.g., N.Y. BUS. CORP. LAW 510(b)). This means that the corporation can not pay out a dividend to its shareholders from the net profits of the accounting period unless the corporation's assets minus its liabilities are greater than the shareholder's contributions (this is known as *stated capital*).

RMBCA	DGCL
§6.40 - Distributions to Shareholders •§6.40 **(a)** Subject to limitations by Articles of Incorporation. •§6.40 **(b)** If no date given for a record of which shareholders are entitled, then it is the date that the distribution is authorized. •§6.40 **(c)** No distribution can be made if afterwards the corporation would be insolvent: •Corporation couldn't pay it debts as they come due in the usual course of business (**Equity Insolvency Test**); or Corporation's total assets would be less than the sum of its total liabilities plus the amount needed to satisfy the preferential rights if the corporation will dissolve. (**Balance Sheet Test**: Total Assets equal or exceed Total liabilities + Dissolution). •§6.40 **(d)** This will be determined by financial statements or by a fair valuation by the Board. •§6.40**(e)** Deals with date for the purchase redemption, etc. •§6.40**(f)** A Corporations' indebtedness is the same as that of any other debtor unless an agreement is made otherwise.	**§170 - Dividends; Payment; Wasting Asset Corporations** •Directors can declare and pay dividends. •Pay out of surplus account or net profits of fiscal year. • Can't pay out dividends if the capital is diminished. • I f a corporation issues notes of debenture as a dividend and at such time the corporation had surplus or net profits from which a dividend could be lawfully paid nothing in §170 will invalidate or otherwise affect such note or debenture. •Any corporation involved in the exploitation of "wasting assets" (patents, natural resources etc.) may determine net profits without taking into consideration the depletion of those assets. **§172 - Liability of Directors as to Dividends or Stock Redemption** •Board members will be fully protected by relying in good faith on records and reports when making a decision as to a distribution or to redeem stock. **§173 - Declaration & Payment of Dividends** •May be paid in cash, property, or shares of stock.

1. Dividend tests:

a) Delaware uses **Nimble Dividends Test:**
Corporation can declare dividends regardless of the impairment of the capital account to be paid:

   i)   Out of current profits; or

   ii) Out of earnings (profits) from current <u>and the preceding</u> year. Not just the current accounting period. DGCL §170.

b)**The Equity Insolvency Test and the Balance Sheet Test:**

RMBCA	DGCL
Official Comment to § 6.40 (very applicable to all statutes) **EQUITY INSOLVENCY TEST** •You can't pay dividends that will hinder ability to pay your debts. •Only concerned with the liquidity of the corporation. •Does not matter in stock dividends. Directors can rely on reports & opinions (§8.30). •This is important to creditors. •Matter of Board judgment. Look at Current Ratio: Current Asset/Current Liabilities (1-2 is good). •Quick Ratio: (Cash + Accounts Receivable)/Current Liabilities	
BALANCE SHEET TESTS •Must use a valid accounting method. •Distributions are prohibited if assets are less than liabilities and the amount of money needed to satisfy liquidation rights of other classes of shares. •Total assets plus dividends must equal the total liabilities. **If dividend fails either test, then unlawful.**	

RMBCA	DGCL
§6.31 - Corporation's Acquisition of Its Own Shares •No more treasury stock since there is no par value; •They become authorized unissued shares; •They cannot be reissued if the articles of incorp. state so, the # of authorized shares is reduced by the # of shares acquired (need amendment to articles of incorp.); •This is a distribution and will be limited by **§ 6.40.**	**§160 - Corporation's Powers Respecting Ownership, Voting, etc. of Its Own Stock;** •Rights of Stock Called for Redemption •Corporation may buy back its own stock as long as the <u>capital of the corporation is not impaired</u>; •They can resell the redeemed shares; •The shares are held in treasury, but not entitled to vote; •The shares are not counted for quorum purposes; •The shares are not counted as outstanding shares for voting purposes. **§ 244 - Reduction of Capital** Corporation can reduce its capital by redemption.

Conversion Rights: The right of exchanging securities, usually preferred shares, for a number of shares of another class, called the *conversion securities.*

2.   Liability for unlawful distributions

1) Directors are generally jointly and severally liable for the full amount of the unlawful distribution unless they can show that they acted diligently and in good faith in making a distribution.

2) Shareholders are often absolutely liable if the corporation is *insolvent or is rendered insolvent* from the dividend.
    • Usually the shareholders will be required to return the distribution for the creditors' benefit. *(See,* e.g., *Wood v. National City Bank,* 24 F.2d 661 (2d Cir. 1928)).

3) If the Corporation is solvent, innocent shareholders will not be held liable and are entitled to keep their dividends.

RMBCA	DGCL

§8.33(a) - Liability for Unlawful Distribution
•Director who votes for or assents to an unlawful dividend or distribution is liable to the creditors upon dissolution.
•Such a director is entitled to contribution from:
  •all other directors who could also be held liable for unlawful distributions; and
  •each shareholder, for the amount accepted knowing that the distribution was unlawful.
• Any proceeding under this section must be commenced within two years of the date of the distribution.
	§174 - Liability of Directors for Unlawful Payment of Dividend
	All directors are jointly and severally liable for the full amount of the dividend paid for six years if there is willful or negligent violation of §160 or §173 in paying stock dividends or making a redemption.
	•A director may exonerate himself from liability if he were absent when the distribution was declared or by entering his dissent in the minute books at the time the dividend was made or immediately thereafter.
	• A director may seek contribution from the other directors or a stockholder who accepted a dividend knowing that it was unlawful.

3. Redemption and repurchase of shares as dividend

Repurchases and redemptions have the same effect as a dividend. They take money away from creditors and are therefore *subject to the same limitations as dividends.*

    a. Most corporations *can redeem* their shares (acquire outstanding shares from shareholders) if the articles of incorporation allow it. This can be done with any available funds.

b. *Repurchases* can only be done if the corporation has surplus and they must:
- (i) The repurchase must serve a corporate purpose.
- (ii) The repurchase can not favor inside shareholders at the expense of outside shareholders *(See Zahn v. Transamerica*, 162 F.2d 36 (3d Cir. 1947)).
- (iii) Redemptions also can not be used by directors to prevent a corporate raid if the sole purpose is to keep the directors in office. *(See Cheff v. Mathis*, 199 A.2d 548 (Del. 1964). However, this rule does not apply if the corporate raid is a threat to the corporations interest as opposed to the directors interest.

IV. RUNNING THE CORPORATION

A. Introduction

The essential idea here is that the corporation, a jurisdictional entity, has to be run by someone or a group of people. Difficult questions arise when the people running the company (those who control) are not those who own the corporation (the shareholders). Thus conflicts often arise (will see later).

B. The Board of Directors

1. Election and removal of the Board.

a. Generally Absent a statutory requirement that the Board seeks shareholder approval, the Board is authorized to take all actions needed to manage a corporation. The Board is protected by the *Business Judgment Rule* in making such decisions and it does not matter if the shareholders merely disagree.
- Shareholders can express their opinions, but they have no binding effect.
- To protect the shareholders, there is a *fiduciary duty* and they can *oust the Board.*
- The power to elect the board is called the *Shareholder Franchise.*

Under the common law, shareholders can only remove directors for cause. Under both the RMBCA and the DGCL shareholders *can remove with or without cause.*

Campbell v. Loew's, Inc., 134 A.2d 852 (Del. 1957)
In Delaware, to remove a director, the director must be given notice and a chance to defend themselves.
Removal cannot be done arbitrarily.

Auer v. Dressel, 118 N.E.2d 590 (N.Y. 1954)
the shareholders have the power to remove the Board and they also have the power to elect new board members.

2. Resignation and removal of directors

Traditionally, shareholders could only remove directors with cause. Today most statutes allow shareholders to remove directors with or without cause.

Directors usually must be given notice of their removal, reasons for removal, as well as a chance to answer the charges made against them before the shareholders. (Due Process).

RMBCA	DGCL
8.07 Resignation of Directors •§ A director must deliver written notice to the board, chairman or corporation. •Effective when delivered unless otherwise specified.	**§141(b)** •A director can resign at any time upon written notice to the corporation.
§8.08 Removal of Directors by Shareholders •Remove with or without cause unless the Articles of Incorporation requires cause; •If director elected by voting group of shareholders, only that voting group may participate in the vote to remove; •If cumulative voting, a director may not be removed if number needed to elect him is against his removal. If not cumulative voting, a director may only be removed if the number of votes for removal is greater than the number of votes against removal; •A director may only be removed by shareholders at a meeting explicitly called for that purpose.	**§141(k)** •A director may be removed, with or without cause, by the majority of the shares then entitled to vote at an election of directors. **Exceptions** •Can't be done if the certificate of incorporation states otherwise; •If cumulative voting & less than entire board is to be removed, no director may be removed without cause if the number against his removal would be sufficient to elect him cumulatively; •If a class is entitled to elect a director, only that class can vote to remove him.

Common Law

Removal for cause (See supra)
> **Auer v. Dressel**, 118 N.E.2d 590 (N.Y. 1954) (which required a hearing by the shareholders when a director is removed with cause).

> **Campbell v. Loew's, Inc.**, 134 A.2d 852 (Del. 1957) (holding that the shareholders have a right to elect directors between annual meetings).

Removal without Cause
> **Rover v. Cotter**, 547 A.2d 603 (Del. 1968) (Holding that a shareholder may amend the certificate of incorporation to allow them to remove a director without cause).

3   Corporate directors, corporate officers and board functioning - Corporate Governance

a.   Corporate Directors

RMBCA	DGCL
§8.03 - Number and Election of Directors •There must be one or more directors as determined by the articles of incorporation or the by-laws. •Changes in board number: • Board may approve changes up to 30% of the board; and • Shareholders must approve changes that are greater than 30%. •The articles or by-laws can set a minimum or maximum number of directors. •The board is elected annually, unless staggered under **§8.06**.	**§121(b)** •The number is fixed by the by-laws or certificate of incorporation. •There must be at least 1 director. •Changes in number are made by amending the certificate of incorporation or the by-laws. •Each director will hold his office until a successor is chosen or removal or resignation.
§8.05 - Terms of Directors Generally •Directors have one-year terms and are elected at the annual shareholder meeting, unless staggered under §8.06 •A decrease in the number of directors does not shorten an incumbent director's term. •Even if a term ends, a director continues to serve unless the number is decreased or a new director is elected. •If a director is elected to fill a vacancy, the term ends at the next annual shareholders meeting.	**141(d)** •Directors serve 1 year terms and are elected at the annual meeting.

RMBCA	DGCL
§8.10 - Vacancy on Board Unless the articles of incorporation states otherwise: •Shareholders may fill the vacancy; •The board may fill the vacancy. 　• If the number of directors is less than quorum, they may fill the vacancy by an affirmative vote of majority remaining; •If a vacant office was held by a director elected by a voting group, only that voting group may vote to fill the vacancy; •A vacancy that will occur at a specific later date may be filled before it occurs, but the new director can't take office until the vacancy occurs.	**§223 - Vacancies and Newly Created Directorships** Unless the Certificate of incorporation states otherwise: •Vacancies and newly created directorships may be filled by a majority of directors then in office-- even if less than quorum; •If there are no directors left, the officers call a special shareholder meeting or ask the court of chancery to order elections under **§211**; •If directors are divided by classes, then the new director filling the vacancy will not hold office until the next class election, or a director resigns, then the directors may fill spot; •If the remaining directors are less than a majority, then 10% of the shares can demand an election to fill the vacancies or replace the directors chosen by the board; •If a director resigns, the majority of the directors (including those who resigned) have the power to fill vacancies. New directors take over when the resignation becomes effective.

C. **Corporate officers**
  1. **Election**
      - Usually done by the Board;
      - Officers hold positions at the Board's pleasure;
      - Officer's can be discharged even if they have a contract with the corporation;
      - Officer's appoint lower level management, who conduct day-to-day operations.
  2. **Fiduciary duty**
      - Officers also have the duties of loyalty and care towards the corporation;
      - Since the officers are responsible for the day to day management of the corporations business, they may be held to a higher standard than an outside director.
  3. **Power to bind** the corporation
      Usually the president (and sometimes other officers) have the power to bind the corporation only for everyday transactions that arise in the ordinary course of business. *See infra* discussing who has the authority to bind the corporation.

RMBCA	DGCL
§8.40 Required Officers •By-laws can describe officers; or Board appoints in accordance with the by-laws; •Officers are allowed to appoint their assistants; •One officer must prepare all board and shareholder meeting minutes; •One person may fill two offices.	**§142 (a)** •The by-laws determine officers' titles and duties. •The Board may make a resolution determining titles or duties as long as it is not inconsistent with the by-laws; •One officer must take minutes of the stockholders' and boards meetings. •One officer can hold multiple offices.
§8.41 Duties of officers •Set forth in the by-laws or prescribed by the board.	

RMBCA	DGCL

8.42 Standards of conduct
•Officers must discharge their duties:
  • In good faith;
  • With the care of an ordinary prudent person in a like position;
  • In a manner he reasonably believes to be in the corporations best interest.
•In doing this, the director may rely on information, opinions, reports, or statements if prepared or presented by:
  • One or more officers or employees whom the officer reasonably believes is competent and reliable;
  • Legal counsel, accountants and other experts as to matters he reasonably believes they have competence.
•If the officer has knowledge making such reliance unwarranted, he is not acting in good faith;
•An officer is not liable for an action taken if performed in compliance with this section.	

§8.43 Resignation & Removal of officers •Resignation is allowed at any time upon delivery of notice and is effective on the delivery date unless the notice states otherwise; •The Board may remove a director at any time with out without cause. **§8.43 Contract Rights** •Neither removal nor resignation affects the officer or the corporations contract rights.	**§142 (b)** •Term lengths are determined by either the by-laws or the Board. •Any officer may resign at any time upon written notice. •An officer holds his position during the term unless there is death, removal or resignation.

D. Board functioning

1) Meetings

    (i)   The Board must hold at least one meeting per year.

    (ii)   The Board will generally hold regular meetings but is allowed to hold special meetings for a particular purpose.

    (iii)   Unless the statute states otherwise, a Board may only act through a meeting.

    (iv)   A meeting can usually occur *through a telephone conference call* (check the specific statute) as long as all members can *simultaneously hear each other.*

    (v)   Most statutes allow the Board to act through *unanimous written consent.*

    (vi)   *Notice, quorum and voting rights* are determined through the statute and the corporation's governing documents. Shareholders are entitled to notice of a meeting.

    (vii)   Quorum requirements prevent a minority of directors from taking actions against the majorities will (*but see* the cumulative voting *discussed infra*, which ensure that the minority shareholders have a voice on the Board);

    (viii) There must be quorum at the time the Board votes-- not just at the beginning of the meeting--therefore, a director can not just walk out to prevent quorum. *See Gearing v. Kelly* 182 N.E.2d 391 (N.Y. 1962) (holding that a director who is purposely absent from a meeting to prevent quorum can not complain if the others take action);

    (ix)   Quorum requirements will often be relevant when the directors are filling Board vacancies. Usually only a majority of the remaining directors is needed. (RMBCA § 8.10(a)(3)).

2) Approval of Transactions

  a) Approval for transactions must be made by the entire
     Board, not an individual director.
  b) This can only be done through a meeting or unanimous
     written consent.

Hypothetical: Suppose something develops and the officers need
Board approval within 24 hours but five (out of nine) board
members are not available? This causes conflict between the
desire to protect the shareholders' interest through the boards'
action and the boards need to act quickly.

The following are issues that the board should analyze:
  Can you have an emergency meeting with only half of the
  Board and on short notice?
  - Look to the by-laws and articles of incorporation.
  - Look to the statutes regarding Board meetings.
  Are there alternatives? YES
  - Action without a meeting.
  - Emergency doctrine.
  How to avoid this problem in the future.
  - Change the quorum number in the by-laws.
  - Reduce notice requirement.
  - Change contract to allow more time.
  - Have small executive committees to handle
    such problems.

3) Board Compensation

  Under most statutes the board may fix reasonable
  compensation. Although this appears to be a conflict
  of interest--the Board determines its own salary. This
  usually is not a problem because the Board will appoint
  a compensation committee to avoid appearance of
  impropriety.

A director who is also an officer of the corporation can be paid in both contexts. However, the director may not participate in the vote to determine his salary as an officer.

4)   Board Committees

a)   Committees can act upon issues arising between board meetings.

b)   If acting within their purpose they can make many decisions instead of the full Board.

c)   Their actions are limited by the statute and the by-laws.

d)   They are often made up of outside directors instead of officer-directors.

e)   They are usually narrowly tailored (e.g. executive committee, compensation committee, nominating committee, audit committee, special committee for a particular transaction).

The RMBCA and the DGCL are almost identical for these sections.

RMBCA	DGCL
§8.20 - Meetings The Board can hold regular or special meetings inside or outside of the state. •Any means of communication may be used including telephone conference calls, as long as they can simultaneously participate and hear each other. (unless the by-laws or articles of incorporation state otherwise) •Any director through this method is present.	**§141 - Number, Qualifications Terms and Quorum; Committees; Classes of Directors; Non-profit Corporations; Reliance upon Books; Action Without Meeting; Removal** •§141 (g) Meetings may be held in or out-of-state; •§141 (i) Any means of communication may be used including telephone conference calls, as long as they can simultaneously participate and hear each other. A director who participates in a meeting through this method is considered present at the meeting.

RMBCA	DGCL
§8.21 - Action without meeting •You can have action without a meeting as long as all members participate. (unless the by-laws or articles of incorporation state otherwise) •Must have **unanimous written consent;** •It must be signed by all and included in the corporate records; •Effective when the last director signs it; •Has the same effect as if voted on in a meeting.	**§141(f)** •May have action without a meeting as long as all members consent in writing, and the writings are filed with the minutes of the proceedings; •Need **unanimous written** consent.
§8.22 - Notice of Meeting •Unless the articles of incorporation state otherwise, you can have **regular** meetings without notice of date, time, place and purpose; •Unless the articles state otherwise, **special meetings** need at least **2 days notice** of date, time and place; •Notice of a special meeting does not need to state a purpose (unless the articles of incorporation or by-laws states otherwise).	**No notice requirement** Look to the by-laws or the certificate of incorporation.
§8.23 - Waiver of Notice •Director may waive the notice requirement; •The waiver must be in writing, signed by the director, and filed with the minutes; •Showing up at the meeting waives notice **unless** the director shows up, objects to the meeting and doesn't vote.	Not applicable.

RMBCA	DGCL
§8.24 - Quorum and Voting •Unless the articles or by-laws state differently, QUORUM is the greater of: • a majority of the fixed number of directors; or • a majority of the members prescribed or in actuality at time of notice. •**Minimum Quorum** required for a legally effective vote is 1/3 of the board ; •There must be an affirmative vote of a majority of those present to act on the proposition unless the by-laws state that you need more; •A present director will be seen as assenting to the proposition unless he: • Objects to holding the meeting at the beginning; • Abstains or votes against the proposition at the meeting and the minutes show the directors dissent or abstention; or • Delivers written notice of dissent at the end of the meeting or shortly thereafter.	**§141(b)** •**Quorum = a majority** of the total number of directors; •The by-laws can decrease this number (unless the certificate of incorporation states otherwise); •This number can never be less than one-third (1/3) of total directors; •The vote of the majority of the directors present when there is quorum is needed unless by-laws state otherwise.
§8.11 Compensation of Directors •The board may fix the directors compensation unless the articles of compensation state otherwise.	**§141(h)** •The board may fix director compensation unless the by-laws or certificate of incorporation states otherwise.

RMBCA	DGCL
§8.25 - Committees	**§141(c) Committees**
• Unless the laws states otherwise, the Board may set up committees with 2 or more members;	• The board can designate committees as long as they are approved by the majority of the directors;
• Committees must be approved by the greater of:	• Committee may exercise all powers and authority of the board except:
• The majority of all directors in office at the time; or	• Amend the certificate of incorporation.
• The number of directors required to take action **under §8.24;**	• Adopt a merger or consolidation agreement.
• **§§8.20 & 8.24** also apply to committees and committee meetings;	• Recommend to the shareholders that they sell, lease or exchange all or substantially all of the corporation's assets.
• The **committee may exercise the Boards' authority** under §8.01 as much as the by-laws state so **except**:	• Recommend a dissolution or revocation of dissolution.
• Authorize distributions.	• Declare a dividend.
• Approve any action that must be approved by shareholders.	• Authorize issuance of stock.
• Fill board vacancies.	
• Amend the articles of incorporation or by-laws.	• (5 & 6 may be done if the by-laws or the certificate of incorporation states so).
• Approve a merger plan not requiring shareholder approval.	
• Authorize or approve reacquisition or sale of shares or "all of the assets."	

Note: DCGL § 141 Committees:

Any corporation formed before July 1, 1996 may elect to be governed by the above DGCL § 141 provisions or the following provisions:

  •   The Board may designate 1 or more committees each consisting of 1 or more directors. The Board may also

71

appoint 1 or more alternate members to replace an absent or disqualified member.

- To the extent provided in the resolution or in the By-laws, any such committee may exercise all powers and authority of the Board except:
    1. Approving, adopting or recommending to stockholders any action or matter expressly required by the DCGL to be submitted to stockholders for approval; or
    2. Adopting amending or repealing any by-law.

5. **Voting Arrangements used to elect and remove directors**. *(See also proxy discussion infra)*

- **Default rules**- top vote getter gets elected;
- **Cumulative voting**- *see discussion infra.*;
- **Pooling arrangement**- private contracts.
  Usually minority shareholders agree to vote a certain way for a certain period or for a certain issue;
- **Voting trusts**- RMBCA § 7.30. Legal title transferred to trustee and Secretary of State;
- **Irrevocable Proxies**;

a) **Cumulative Voting** -- and how the majority may curtail:

RMBCA	DGCL
§7.28- Usually voting is plurality however, corporations may choose to have the right to cumulative voting; •Shares can only be voted cumulatively if: • The meeting notice states so; • Shareholder gives 48 hour notice of intent to cumulate votes.	§214 •Do not need to have cumulative voting, but it can put it in the articles of incorporation.

(i) **Cumulative voting** - to ensure that there is *minority representation* on the Board. It concerns only voting, not any other aspect of corporate governance. In most states cumulative voting is permissive rather than mandatory.

- In these states even if the by-laws or articles of incorporation allow cumulative voting, it can be removed by amending the articles or by-laws.
- In some states, cumulative voting is mandatory and exists even if it is not mentioned in the articles or by-laws. (*See, e.g.,* CAL. CORP. CODE § 708).

(ii) **How cumulative voting works**:

Each share is entitled to *one vote for each share of stock for each director* that must be elected.

Therefore, if there are 3 open spots on the board and a shareholder owns 10 shares, she has 30 votes in total (10 for each director). This shareholder can use these votes any way she wishes--meaning she can cast all 30 votes for one nominee or spread them amongst as many nominees as she wishes.

However, the minority shareholders will be best served if they concentrate their votes on one or two directors. The arithmetic ensures that the minority will be able to elect one or more directors if they concentrate their votes. (If there was no cumulative voting, the majority would always have the most votes and be allowed to elect the entire Board).

(iii) **Formula**:
$$Y = \frac{s \times d}{D+1} + 1$$

Y = Number of shares required to elect director;

s = Number of shares represented at the meeting;

d = Number of directors it is desired to elect; and

D = Total number of directors to be elected.

Total Votes per Shareholder = # shares times the # directors

b) **Cumulative Voting and how the Majority can Curtail**

Staggered/Classified voting- each Shareholder is allowed a certain number of seats to elect on the Board.

(1) **Staggered Board:**
- A staggered board is where the Board is divided into groups of directors and each group has a different term.
- This provides that only a percentage of the Board (as opposed to the entire Board) is up for election at each annual meeting. This, in turn, assures continuity on the Board from year to year and allows the majority to avoid minority representation from cumulative voting.

Some states prohibit staggering boards when cumulative voting is mandatory (*See, e.g.,* CAL CORP. CODE § 301*; see also Wolfson v. Avery*, 126 N.E.2d 701 (Ill. 1955) (holding that cumulative voting prohibits classified Boards); *but see Bohanaon v. Corporation. Com.*, 313 P.2d 379 (Ariz. 1957).

RMBCA	DGCL
§8.06 Staggered Terms for Directors •If the board consists of 9 or more directors, the articles of incorporation may provide for staggered terms; •There should be 2-3 groups each with 1/2 - 1/3 of the total number of directors in each group.	**§141(d)** •There can be 1,2, or 3 classes; •The first expires in year 1, the second in year 2 and the third in year 3, but they will each have 3 year terms after the initial term. Thus a new board will be elected every three years.

(2) The **Majority can remove minority** elected directors.

- This is usually not allowed when there is cumulative voting. If the number of votes against removing a director is enough to elect him through cumulative voting, he can't be removed. (*See, e.g.*, RMBCA § 8.08(c); DGCL § 141(k). (only applies for removal without cause).

(3) **Classified Boards**
- The articles of incorporation may specify that certain classes of stock may elect a determined number of directors. For example, if there are three classes of common shareholders; class 1, 2, and 3. The Articles may specify that class 1 shareholders may elect 4 directors, class 2 shareholders may elect 2 directors and class 3 shareholders may elect 1 director. In essence, class 1 controls the corporation.

(4) **Change in the Board Size**
- Reducing the size of the Board would decrease minority representation because more shares would be needed to ensure a seat.
- However, the corporation can require a greater percentage of shareholders to approve such an action (80% instead of a majority), thereby preventing the majority from reducing the number of directors.

Blasius Industries, Inc. v. Atlas Corporation, 564 A.2d 651 (Del. 1988)
   Facts: Blasius owned 9.1% of Atlas corporation. He wanted the board to restructure and increase the number of directors so as to dilute the power of the board. The board disagreed and decreased its size in an emergency meeting to prevent his plan.

   Held: The Board does not have the power to bypass the importance of the *corporate franchise.*
- The board cannot prevent the shareholders from voting, even if the board is acting in good faith.

- The franchise is of paramount importance breaching it is a *breach of the duty of loyalty.*
- Shareholders have the right to act even if it is not for the best according to the Board.

Solution: Send information to the shareholders using corporate funds to tell them why the Board disagrees with the plan.

E.   **How the Board of Directors Runs the Corporation: Overview of Duties and Protections**

The Business Judgment Rule (BJR): allows the board to run the company without undue interference.

1. **Business Judgment Rule** - A device by the courts that protects decisions made by a reasonably prudent director as long there is *informed judgment.* There is only liability for gross negligence or illegal acts.
   This rule creates a rebuttable presumption that business decisions made upon reasonable information and with some rationality do not give rise to directors' liability even if they turn out badly or disastrously from the standpoint of the corporation.

   Reasons for limiting liability:
   - A certain amount of innovation and risk-taking is essential if businesses are to grow and prosper.
   - Directors, like executives, must constantly engage in a risk/return calculations.
   - Imposing greater director liability would make directors a form of "cost spreaders."

   Note: There is no Business Judgment Rule protection for Duty of Loyalty violations.

2. **Duty of Loyalty**

   Duty of Loyalty - when private interests conflict with the corporation interests, the corporation interests must prevail. Directors must subordinate their interests to the corporation.

a. **No self dealing** under the Duty of Loyalty:
   - Directors self interest must not unduly influence the decision of the corporation. (cannot profit personally --)
   - Directors must give full and fair disclosure of any conflicts of interest.

b. **No excessive compensation or waste.**
   Generally, directors may not collect excessive $. But, no such restriction on officers (CEO's, CFO's, etc.), although this is a subject of debate.

c. **No seizing the corporate opportunity**
   "Corporate Opportunity Doctrine" (*See infra* for in depth discussion).
   - Applies to directors and controlling shareholders.
   - Directors or shareholders must give any business opportunity that properly belongs to the corporation to that corporation.

   However, the *Line of Business Test* can be used to see if there is corporate opportunity. If not, the director can get involved with that opportunity.

d. **Line of Business Test (LBT)**
   If a business opportunity is within the corporations "area" of dealing, such business opportunity must be pursued by officers and the Board for the corporation and not for themselves.

3. **Duty of Care** - The directors must perform their job as an ordinary prudent and diligent person in a like position under similar circumstances. If they do so then their actions will be protected by the **Business Judgment Rule**. It is rare that this duty is breached. Only in cases of breach of duty of honesty is it enforced. Generally,

directors should act reasonably in managing their own affairs.

The director is only liable if there is gross negligence or recklessness thereby removing him from the protection of the **Business Judgment Rule.**

a. There are two types of due care:
   (i) Decision is made must not be suspect; and
   (ii) The *second* is substantive. The subject of the transaction must not be inherently negligent.

RMBCA	DGCL
§8.30 Business Standard Test **A director shall discharge his duties in good faith:** •With the care of an ordinary prudent person in a like position; •In a manner that he reasonably believes to be in the companies best interest; **In doing so, the director may rely on information, opinions and reports or statements if prepared by:** •*Officers*--if he reasonably believes they are reliable and competent. *Experts*--accountants, lawyers, etc. •*Committees of directors* that the director is not a member of; A director is not personally liable for any actions if he performed his duties in compliance with this section.	**§141(e)** **A board member is fully protected for relying on in good faith:** • Corporate records; • Opinions, reports, statements made by an officer, employee board committee member or any other person he reasonably believes is an expert and has competence.

Note: There is also a duty to act lawfully -- although it would seem such a duty could be simply mentioned in passing under Duty of Care.

4. Duties of shareholders *(see also proxy discussion infra)*

Generally, shareholders have no duty to the corporation unless they are controlling shareholders.

> *Bayer v. Beran*, 49 N.Y.S. 2d 2 (N.Y. Sup. Ct. 1944)
> It is not improper to appoint relatives to responsible positions in a company as long as it is done within the duty of care and does not violate the business judgment rule. A director must use the kind of judgment that one would expect and give in similar situation to the conduct of his own affairs.
>
> *The Business Judgment Rule* requires undivided loyalty and the avoidance of the temptation of self interest.

> *Gamble v. Queens County Water Co.*, 25 N.E. 201 (N.Y. Sup. Ct. 1890)
> A director who is also a shareholder built pipes for $69,000 and sold them to the company for $110,000 after the shareholders approved the transaction. A dissenter sued claiming there was a conflict of interest.
>
> **Held**: There was not a conflict of interest.
> The director as a shareholder owes no duty to the other shareholders when he is voting his stock. He is solely representing himself and his own stock.

Exception

RMBCA § 7.21(b)	• When a corporation holds shares **in** a company as a fiduciary. Majority shareholders have a fiduciary duty.

F. The Duty of Loyalty in Depth

There is no need to decide whether an opportunity belongs to a member of the board or to the corporation if there is no duty of loyalty. Stated differently, it is a breach of a director's duty of loyalty to appropriate a corporate opportunity for him or herself.

Corporate law allows *self dealing* as long as it is fair. Sometimes it is impossible to avoid this to get good business opportunities.

Once a party challenging a transaction has shown that there is a conflict of interest, the burden of showing the transaction is proper rests with the director. However, if the director has proven that the action was disinterested, then the burden falls upon the accusing party.

1. Terms:

Direct Self Interest - Where the director is a party to the deal on both sides; this places a risk on the transaction (RMBCA 8.60(1)(I)).

Indirect Self Interest - When there is someone on the other side of the transaction with whom the director has a strong personal or financial interest; such as relatives, or in other corporations where the director is a director on both sides (RMBCA 8.60(1)(ii)).

2. Rules when Deals by an Interested Director are Permitted: (Different tests from the courts)

Different Tests when Directors interest in the deal must always be disclosed to the Board:
   a. *Substantive fairness plus disinterested Board approval* - If the deal is fair to the corporation and a majority of the disinterested Board members approve of it, then it is valid.
   b. *Court determined substantive fairness* - A transaction with an interested director will be valid if a court determines it was fair on its merits, whether or not it was approved by disinterested directors.
   c. *Fairness or disinterested Board approval* - One or the other; it must be fair on the merits or approved by the majority of the disinterested directors.
   d. *After full disclosure to the Board,* if the Board approves the deal the directors interest is then fully disclosed to the shareholders in good faith.
   e. *Shareholder ratification* - Self dealing is valid if it is approved or ratified by a majority of shareholders.

3.   **Nonvoidability Statutes RMBCA § 8.31; DGCL § 144**

RMBCA	DGCL

§8.31 - Director Conflict of Interest
•The transaction should not be void for the sole reason that the director is a party on both sides if:
  • Material facts are disclosed to the disinterested directors who approve the transaction; or
  • The material facts are disclosed to the shareholders who approve the transaction; or
  • A judge determines it to be fair.
	§144 - Interested Directors; Quorum
	•The transaction should not be void for the sole reason that the director is a party on both sides if:
	  • Material facts are disclosed to the disinterested directors who approve the transaction; or
	  • The material facts are disclosed to the disinterested shareholders who approve in good faith the transaction; or
	  • A judge determines it to be fair.

4 . Judicial Fairness Test:

a. Is the transaction within the range of reasonableness
particularly in price? (Not limited to a single number); and
b. Is it valuable to the corporation?

If a court finds that the corporation's interest outweighs those
of the interested director, then, the transaction is acceptable.
Even if fully informed disinterested directors approve the
transaction, you still need to pass the *Judicial Fairness Test.*
Transactions between a person who is a director on both sides
of the deal is subject to less scrutiny then those transactions
where the director seems to be acting in his own personal
interest and is only on one side.

Entire Fairness - Not only do you need fair price, you
also need fair dealing *See Weinberger v. UOP, Inc.*, 457 A.2d
701 (Del. Super. Ct. 1983).
 - Full disclosure so that the Board can really review it on
the merits.
 - Nondisclosure and approval - Failure of the fairness
test, such as withholding information by a director, will
rescind a transaction.

RMBCA	DGCL
§8.31	**§144(a)**
You need a majority of directors (more than 1) without interest for approval they are defined as:	You need a majority of directors (more than 1) without interest for approval who:
• Cannot be directly or indirectly interested in the transaction;	• Cannot be directly or indirectly interested in the transaction;
• Cannot be dominated by the interested director (more than merely being dominated is required for domination, it is acting as the dominator requests without independent judgment).	• Cannot be dominated by the interested director (more than merely being dominated is required for domination, it is acting as the dominator requests without independent judgment).

5.   **Shareholder Ratification of Self Dealing Transactions**

a. If a majority of votes are cast by shareholders that are disinterested and fully informed, then the courts will uphold the transaction. The burden will shift to the plaintiff to prove:
  (i)   The transaction constituted waste:
         No person of sound business judgment would find that the consideration was fair;
  (ii)   Shareholders were uninformed; and
  (iii) Transaction was illegal.

b. Courts are weary about self-dealing transactions if shareholder ratification is by a majority of shareholders who were interested in the transaction.

c. If by a unanimous vote the shareholders ratify self-dealing, then it cannot be set aside, as long as there was full disclosure.

G. Corporate Opportunity Doctrine:

a. **General Rule**: A director or officer cannot seize a corporate opportunity for his own benefit unless the corporation consents because of the Duty of Loyalty. The rule arises out of the director's duty of loyalty to the corporation.

(1) A corporate opportunity means that the corporation would have taken it if it had the chance.

(2) There is no need to present the opportunity to the Board if it is a natural increment in the director's business outside of the corporation. This would be a proper expansion of his preexisting interests.

(3) The director owes the corporation the first right to acquire the opportunity on the same basis that the director would be entitled to do so.

(4) Corporate Opportunities refers to, a director or others with a close relationship to the corporation, taking advantage of information acquired from the corporation.

(5) The corporate opportunity fiduciary concept must be looked into to see if it would be unfair for the director to exploit the opportunity.
There is a tension between two factors:
i. Management should not compete with the corporation for business.
ii. Management should not be hindered from developing new business.

(6) Two questions the director must ask when presented with a corporate opportunity:
i. When does a business opportunity belong to the corporation?
ii. How can the corporation consent to the director taking the opportunity?

b. **Tests** Used to Determine if an Opportunity is, In Fact the Corporations

1) **Assets**
A fiduciary cannot develop a business opportunity using the corporation's assets.
What are corporate assets?
> Cash
> Employees
> Property or other facilities
> Customer list
> Trade secrets

If the director does develop a business opportunity with the corporation's assets, the director is *liable even if the corporation had no identifiable interest in the opportunity.*

If the opportunity was discovered by the director while he was acting in his capacity as a director then it also belongs to the corporation.

2) **Expectancy test**
A business opportunity belongs to the corporation if the corporation has a legal interest or expectancy in the opportunity, or if it is a necessary opportunity for the corporation to continue its business.

Farber v. Servan Land Co., Inc., 662 F.2d 371
Facts: Even though they had not yet voted, there was still interest in the deal by the stockholders.
Held: The ratification by the Board members was not sufficient because the interested directors voted. The stockholders were not completely informed. This was a corporate opportunity because the corporation had an interest in the land. Extension onto the land was in the natural interest of the corporation.

Nebraska Power Co. v. Koenig, 139 N.W. 839
(Neb. 1913)
Held: corporation had an expectancy interest in the rights
to divert water from a stream when the continuous flow of
water was necessary for the businesses' success.

See also Pike's Peak Co. v. Pfunter, 123 N.W. 19 (Mich.
1909) (holding that a corporation has an expectancy or
interest in purchasing or renewing the lease in land that it
had leased).

3) **Line of Business Test**
    A business opportunity is a corporate opportunity if:
    1. The corporation has knowledge, experience and the
       ability to pursue it; and
    2. The opportunity is closely related to the business
       the corporation is already engaged in or may
       reasonably be expected to engage in.

See Miller v. Miller, 222 N.W.2d 71 (Minn. 1947)
    (holding that once it is determined that the opportunity
    falls under the corporation's line of business, the
    director has the burden to prove that she did not violate
    a fiduciary duty in taking the opportunity for personal
    benefit); *see also Guth v. Loft*, 5 A.2d 503 (Del. Ch.
    1939) (holding that a corporation had an expectancy in
    the trademark and secret formula for Pepsi).

Minority view

Burg v. Horn, 380 F.2D 897 (2ND CIR. 1967)
    Facts: Parties were partners in a real estate
    corporation. The defendant had been involved in
    real estate before forming the corporation. There was
    no agreement that all opportunities that came his way
    must be given to the corporation. He purchased an

87

apartment building individually and his partners sued him for breaching the corporate opportunity doctrine. **Held**: Real estate was the defendant's line of business before he entered into a partnership; therefore, no corporate opportunity was stolen.

4) **A.L.I. Principles § 5.05(b):**

Corporate opportunity is defined as:

> A director or senior executive becomes aware of an opportunity in his corporate capacity. The director uses the corporate opportunity for own self interest when they should know that the outsider is offering the opportunity to the corporation; or
> - The director or senior executive became aware of the opportunity through the use of corporate information and should know that the corporation would be interested; or
> - The senior executive knows that the opportunity is closely related to the corporations current or expected business.

A director or senior executive may not take a corporate opportunity for himself unless:
- The corporate opportunity has been *offered*, disclosing all material facts known, including any and all conflicts of interest; *and*
- The opportunity is *rejected* by the corporation by:
    1. Majority of disinterested directors acting under the business judgment rule; or
    2. Majority of disinterested shareholders, provided it is not a waste of corporate assets; or
    3. The taking was fair to the corporation if not ratified or approved.

c.   Different Standards for Inside and Outside Directors

Only insiders are responsible for the Line of Business Test, but both insiders and outsiders are Responsible for the Expectancy Test.

A corporate opportunity only exists for an outside director who is not a full time officer or employee if:

   a)   It is offered to the director with the intent that it be communicated to the corporation; or

   b)   The director obtains the opportunity through corporate information, property or in performance of duties.
        See Klinicki v. Lundgren, 695 P.2d 906 (OR. 1985).

d.   Special Problems in Corporate Opportunity Doctrine:

Allocation when a director is tied to more than one corporation Factors to consider:

   a)   Look to see if the opportunity came to the director through the corporations information or through the director's service to the corporation.

   b)   Is one corporation already in that line of business, or will that line of business be a natural extension to the corporations line of business?

   c)   Look to see which corporation the director owes a primary duty of loyalty to?

        •   A person has a greater duty of loyalty to the corporation where he is a full time officer than the corporation where he is only an outside director. (*See* A.L.I. § 5.05).

Johnsten v. Greene, 1231 A.2d 919 (Del. 1956) (holding that a person who is an outside director for many corporations can give the business opportunity to any of them or keep it for himself as long as it was offered in his individual capacity and it is not closely related to any particular corporation's business).

e.   **Remedies for Violating the Corporate Opportunity Doctrine**

   (1)   **Imposition of a constructive trust**
   A director will hold it for the corporations benefit (*See, e.g., Klinicki discussed supra); But see Lincoln Stores v. Grant,* 3 N.E.2d 704 (Mass. 1941) (holding that a constructive trust will only be imposed if the property acquired is one that the director knew the corporation needs or intends to acquire).

   (2)   **Remedies:**
      (i)   Compensation to the corporation for lost profits and damages.
      (ii)   Return to the corporation profits earned through the opportunity.
      (iii)   Give the opportunity to the corporation.

f.   **Consent test for activity considered corporate opportunities:**

   (1)   **Voluntary consent**- Many courts hold that it is best for the corporation to have a *voluntary fairness review* by disinterested directors and/or shareholders. The review must provide:
      a)   Full Disclosure to the Board; and
      b)   Disclose the interest or conflict of interest;

   Consent, as relied upon in a voluntary fairness review, is valid if a disinterested board does not take it. *(See Kerrigan v. Unity savings Association,* 317 N.E.2d 39 (Ill. 1974));
   If the director does not fully disclose the opportunity and allows the corporation to reject it, he has not obtained valid consent.

(2) **Implied consent:**

    (1) The corporation has deemed to consent to the taking if it is unable to take the opportunity for itself.

    (2) A director can not rely on the corporation's financial inability to pursue the opportunity.

- If the corporation did not have the funds, it is not necessarily an implied consent, because it may be in a position to raise the money; except in the event that the corporation is insolvent. *See Klinicki v. Lundgren*, 695 P.2d 906 (Or. 1985).

- A director may be held to have a conflict of interest because he failed to use "best efforts" to obtain funds. *See Irving Trust Co. v. Deutsch*, 73 F.2d 121 (2d Cir 1934); *see also A.C. Petters Co. v. St. Cloud Enterprises, inc.*, 222 N.W.2d 83 (Minn. 1974) (holding that a director is not required to advance personal funds, but must make a good faith effort to locate funds for the corporation).

H. The Duty of Care in Depth

1. Generally

Most modern statutes are modeled after the common law which require that directors inform themselves prior to making a business decision and that someone seeking to challenge a decision must show that the director failed to act in good faith, in the honest belief that the action was in the corporation's best interest and on an informed basis. *See Aronson v. Lewis*, 473 A.2d 805 (Del. 1984).

While the duty of care is a high standard, directors are rarely found to violate it because of the *Business Judgment Rule.*

2. Statutes

RMBCA

§ 8.30 - General Standards for Directors (*See also* **DGCL 141(e)**)
Directors Must Perform Their Functions:

• Good faith - Not condone illegal activity;

• In a manner they reasonably believe is in the best interest of the corporation Substantive review; The board's actions must further the corporation's interest.

• With the care of an ordinary prudent person in a like situation.
Informed decision making; Minimal skills or expertise required; Monitor & supervise management;

• In doing so, a director can rely on reports, opinions and statements from reliable sources;

• A director is not liable for any action taken as a director if duties are performed in reliance on this section.

---

3. **The Business Judgment Rule (BJR)**

    Generally Protects the Directors from Breach of the Duty of Care, subject only to Duty of Care and Duty of Loyalty violations.

    The BJR:
    a) Assumes directors acted within the Duty of Care unless it is overcome.
    b) Shields directors from personal liability.
    c) Insulates corporate decisions:
        - We want the Board to take business risks to gain profit, sometimes they fail;
        - Encourages qualified people to serve on Boards without being judged in hindsight.
    d) The Business Judgment Rule is rarely overcome. A Board's decisions will generally be upheld unless it can be shown that the Board acted negligently or in a self interested manner. (*See Gries Sports Enterprises, Inc. v. Cleveland Browns Football Co.*, 496 N.E.2d 959 (Ohio 1986).

    Conflict of interest can arise in any action which the director is personally interested or involved, and may cause the loss of BJR protection.

4. **Where the BJR will not apply:**

    A Party alleging breach of Duty of Care must overcome the Business Judgment Rule presumption. *The plaintiff must prove* either:
    i)   Fraud, illegality, or conflict of interest;
    ii) Lack of a rational business purpose; or
    iii) Gross negligence.

a. Fraud, illegality, conflict of interest

- *Fraud-* any fraudulent action taken by a director may be invalidated, even if fair to corporation.
- *Illegality-* any illegal action, perpetrated or approved by the director overcomes the BJR even if the illegality benefits the corporation.
- *Conflict of interest-* The liability will depend on fairness of the transaction to the corporation.

Duty to Act Lawfully:

Miller v. AT&T, 507 F.2d 759 (3d Cir. 1974)
Facts: A Shareholder brought a derivative action against the corporation for failure to collect funds from the Democratic National Committee, an illegal act violating a federal communications statute.
Held: The Business Judgment Rule can not protect an illegal act unless the director can show a legitimate business purpose.

Note: Had the act not violated the statute, the Director's actions would have been protected by the Best Judgment Rule.

b. Lack of a Rational Business Purpose

Rational Purpose Test- if at the time the decision was made it was "removed from the realm of reason" then the action falls outside of BJR. As long as the corporation may receive a benefit the action is within the BJR.

Rational purpose test:
1. Must be within the realm of reason;
2. Some benefit to the corporation;
3. Rarely found irrational. (*See, e.g., Sinclair Oil v. Levien,* 280 A.2d 7171 (Del. 1971)).

But note: Inaction of Board is a deliberate policy, and is outside of BJR if it was a conscious decision not to act (i.e., such as no action to comply with environmental or antitrust laws). However, if the Board decides to do nothing on Good Faith because the law seemed unwarranted or not applicable then the Director is still protected by BJR.

c. **Director Negligence:**

Rule: Negligence is generally not enough. Only *gross negligence* will do.

If the directors rely on the presumption that the officers and employees are honestly conducting their business they will be protected.

Graham v. Allis Chambers Manufacturing Co., 188 A.2d 125 (Del. Ch. 1963)
Facts: Employees were engaging in activities that violated the antitrust laws. The Directors, who were unaware of this, chose not to implement an antitrust compliance program since there was no grounds to suspect it was needed .
Held: The Directors did not violate the duty of care. In a large corporation, the power is decentralized and management does not participate in each step. If the directors had no actual knowledge, they are *entitled to rely on the honesty and integrity of their subordinates until they have suspicions.*

Bates v. Dresser, 251 U.S. 524 (1920)
Facts: A Bank suffered losses over a 3 year period.
Losses were caused by employee theft. Neither the
President nor the Directors made inquiries into the
thefts even though the President had warning signs of
problems.
Held: The President, but not the Director, was liable.
His failure to take affirmative action or make inquiry
after he knew of the thefts breached his duty of care to
the corporation. The Directors were not liable because
their failure to act was more reasonable. They didn't
supervise the daily corporate operations and were
reasonable in relying on the President. they had no
reason to make inquiries.

A.L.I. 4.01-duty of directors under BJR
The directors only need to make an inquiry if the
situation alerts a reasonable director of the need for an
inquiry.

Do not be passive - The Board must be reasonably
concerned about effective procedures to ensure that they
have not overlooked anything.

Directors must monitor the corporation for
mismanagement. However, a bad business decision,
or poor business judgment *is* acceptable under A.L.I.
401.

Kamin v. American Express, 383 N.Y.S. 2d.
807 (Sup. Ct. 1976)
Facts: The board declared a special dividend to the
shareholders (causing a large tax liability) instead of
liquidating a bad investment. The shareholders brought
a derivative suit claiming a waste of the corporate
assets.

Held: Declaring the dividend is a board decision that is protected by the Business Judgment Rule. The court will only interfere if there was a lack of good faith. The fact that a decision was poor or less advantageous than an alternative is irrelevant.

d. Gross Negligence

Management abuse - The directors have a duty to monitor management abuse.

Francis v. United Jersey Bank, 432 A.2d 814 (N.J. 1981)
Facts: A woman became a director of a bank after her husband (was an officer) died. She was sick and had little knowledge of a bank's business. She relied on her sons' advice which led the bank to bankruptcy.

Held: The director was liable for misappropriation of funds because she had a duty to be informed and to take action. If she had been at all active she, would have caught her sons' illegalities. Here failure to do anything was grossly negligent and a breach of her duty of care.

See also Cede & Co. v. Technicolor Inc., 643 A.2d 345 (Del. 1991) (holding that once a director has been shown to breach the duty of care through inadequate inquiry, the director has the duty to show the lack of causation of the shareholder's injuries).

Rules for Directors
To avoid being grossly negligent:
- If a director feels he should not be a director because he does not have the skills, then he must obtain them or quit.

- Directors have an obligation to be informed. (*See infra Smith v. Van Gorkom*).
- Must have at least a rudimentary knowledge of the business of the corporation.
- Directors must attend meetings.
- Be familiar with the finances.
- Report illegal action.

While most cases will protect a director from a breach of the Duty of Care, the recent trend is for courts to be very strict in analyzing a director's conduct. The following case is a rare situation that holds a director liable for failure to be adequately informed.

Smith v. Van Gorkom, 488 A.2d 858 (Del. 1985)
Facts: The CEO went to a friend to initiate a merger deal. He offered this friend a low price--$55/share. No negotiations occurred at any point. Many of the terms of the deal were disadvantageous to the corporation-- Senior management was vocal about their disagreement with the deal. The deal was kept very quiet, even the lawyers were uninformed. The CEO told the board about the deal but they never saw it in writing. The corporation had 90 days to accept other offer, but no solicitations were made. The board signed the merger document without reading it even though there existed almost no information that this was a good price or deal. The shareholders approved the merger (Doesn't count because *shareholders cannot ratify violation of fiduciary duty*). (Rule 14a-9)).

Held: The directors violated their duty of care in this transaction.

   a) Blind reliance by the Board will not be protected (DGCL §141(e)). Reliance is OK if it is sound, but, here the board:

      (i)   Never asked where price came from.

      (ii) Never asked who initiated the deal.

      (iii) Made no inquiry into the price or terms of the deal.

  b) Although the board was made up of skilled businessmen, they are not protected.

To be protected, the *directors must ask questions* -- Do not blindly rely on information

Note: All directors are jointly and severally liable unless, under the statutory rules, they dissent to the decision (RMBCA § 8.24).

I.   Limitations on the Board's liability

The limitations on liability will usually only apply when the director is acting in an official capacity for the corporation.

- Becoming a director is risky; consequently, there are systems that will protect directors so that they will accept such positions.
- A problem is that the protection may remove the incentive that the fiduciary duties give to act responsibly. However, corporate decision makers will not bear risks if they are not so protected.

1.   Statutory protections:

RMBCA	DGCL
§2.02(b)(4) - Articles of Incorporation Allows the charter to limit (or eliminate) directors' liability to the corporation of shareholders for money damages for action or omission taken as a director except: •for the amount of financial benefit he received and is not entitled to; • intentional infliction of harm on the corporation or shareholders; • approving illegal distributions (**§8.33**); or •intentional violation of criminal law.	**§102(b)(7) - Contents of Certificate of Incorporation** Allows the charter to limit (or eliminate) personal liability of director to the corporation or shareholder for monetary damages for breach of a fiduciary duty as a director except: (b)(7)(i) for a breach of the duty of loyalty (Note: this provision is not in RMBCA); (b)(7)(ii) for acts or omissions not in good faith or involving intentional misconduct or knowing violation of law (this provision is not in RMBCA); (b)(7)(iii) illegal distributions under § 174; or (b)(7)(iv) any transaction from which the director derived personal benefit.

a) These statutes only apply to liability for monetary damages. They have no effect on availability of equitable relief for breach of fiduciary duties.

b) The statutes require shareholders to affirmatively adopt any exculpatory provision in the articles of incorporation--the limitations will not occur if they are not explicitly adopted.

c) Other methods:
- Some statutes set a liability cap at $100,000 or an annual salary, whichever is greater. *(see e.g.,* Vir. Corp. Code Ann. § 13.1-690).
- Sets a higher standard of culpability for directors' liability; willful or reckless rather than merely gross negligence.
  ALI says that the amount can never be reduced below a years salary.

2. Corporate indemnification

a. Mandatory indemnification for successful defense

RMBCA	DGCL
§8.52 Mandatory Indemnification •Unless limited by the articles of incorporation. •Mandates indemnification of reasonable expenses and attorney fees when a director has been successful on the merits or otherwise in a suit. •A director must be wholly successful in order to be indemnified.	**§145 - Indemnification of Officers, Directors Employees and Agents; Insurance** • Mandatory indemnification of reasonable expenses and attorney fees when a *director* has been successful on the merits or otherwise in a suit. • Available in both criminal and civil. • A director may be only partially successful in a claim or issue and still be indemnified.

(i) **Merits or otherwise** - This means indemnification on the facts or procedurally, not for a settlement out of court. *See, e.g., Waltuch v. Conti Community Services, Inc.*, 833 F. Supp. 302 (S.D.N.Y. 1993).

Extent successful

Merritt Chapman & Scott Corp. v. Wolfson, 321 A.2d 138 (Del. 1974)
A director was charged with five criminal charges. He pleaded no contest to one and the others were dropped. This is seen as partial success; therefore, indemnification is allowed under the DGCL.

Note: Under the RMBCA, *complete nonliability is required*, so the director would not be indemnified. The director must be "wholly successful."

Note: Under DGCL § 145(c) To the extent successful or otherwise, *a present or former director* shall be indemnified against all expenses actually or reasonably incurred.

b. Permissive indemnification for an unsuccessful defense

Directors are not automatically entitled to indemnification--usually the by-laws or articles of incorporation will specify.

Third Party Action (i.e., when an environmental group or government organization sues the corporation or its directors or a director face a criminal action).

c. **Indemnification in actions by or on behalf of the corporation**

Includes shareholder derivative suits brought on behalf of the corporation.

Look to the statutes listed under permissive indemnification for third party actions for the rules of the coverage, criteria and procedure.

	RMBCA	DGCL
Indemnification Criteria	§8.51(a) •If a director conducted himself in good faith; and • The director believes his conduct was in the corporation's best interest or at least not opposed to it; and The director had no reasonable cause to believe that his conduct was unlawful (in criminal cases), then he must be indemnified.	§145(a) •The director must have acted in good faith. •The director believes conduct was in corporation's best interest or at least not opposed to it. •The director must have no reasonable cause to believe that his conduct was unlawful (in criminal cases). •No mandatory statutory indemnification for employees or agents. Indemnification may be granted under charter, by-law, contract or board resolution.
Coverage	§8.51(e), §8.50(3),(4) •A director in a 3rd party suit can be indemnified for reasonable litigation expenses, personal liability and fines or penalties.	§145(a) A director in a 3rd party suit can be indemnified for reasonable litigation expenses and personal liability and fines or penalties including attorney fees.

	RMBCA	**DGCL**
Determination of whether a Director is Entitled to Coverage	§8.55(b) •The board members who are not a party to the action determine indemnification if there is a quorum (of directors who are not a party to the action); •By the shareholders other than the directors seeking to be indemnified (if they are also shareholders); or A committee of non-party directors can name a special independent legal council to determine if the criteria are met (only if there is not a quorum of directors).	§145(d) •Determination of entitlement of indemnification for employees or agents to be made by directors, stockholders or independent counsel, who are not parties to the action (there is no quorum requirement); •Such determination may be made by a committee of non-party directors who can name special independent legal council to determine if the criteria are met.
Case by Case Procedure	§8.55(a) •Can't indemnify under §8.51 unless authorization within the specific case after a determination is made that the indemnification is reasonable. Look at the specific case; doesn't matter if blanket indemnification is in a contract or the by-laws, indemnification is not guaranteed.	§145(d) •Determination of indemnification for director can only be made after it has been determined that indemnification is proper because the director met the requirements of (a).

	RMBCA	DGCL
Case by Case Procedure	**§8.58** •The statute is controlling; indemnification by the shareholders, by-laws, or resolution is invalid if inconsistent; The statute can't be broadened, it can only be narrowed.	**§145(f)** •Indemnification can be given in contract or under the by-laws, as long as consistent with public policy; Allows indemnification to be broadened by charter, by-laws or contract.

RMBCA	DGCL

§8.51(d)
•A corporation may not indemnify director:
  •where the director was adjudged liable to the corporation; or
  •where the director was adjudged liable on the basis that personal benefit was improperly received by him.
Otherwise, the director would be evading liability at the expense of whom he owes it.
 	
*However, if it is merely a settlement, then the director can be indemnified.
	§145(b)
	•No indemnification shall be made when a director has been adjudged to be liable to the corporation unless the court, in view of all circumstances, finds that director is fairly and reasonably entitled to indemnification.
	
	Otherwise, the director would be evading liability at the expense of whom he owes it.
	
	*However, if it is merely a settlement, then the director can be indemnified.
	1

d. Court ordered indemnification

The court has discretionary power in some cases to order indemnification even if the corporation can't or doesn't.

RMBCA	DGCL

§8.54
•Unless the articles of incorporation provide otherwise, a court may order indemnification:
  •If a director is entitled to mandatory indemnification under **§8.52**; and
  •If the director is fairly and reasonably entitled to indemnification whether or not adjudged liable.
 	
•If the director is adjudged liable and to have acted for personal gain, only the expenses can be indemnified.
	§ 145(b)
	• Court may order indemnification "If the director is fairly and reasonably entitled to indemnification in view of all of the relevant circumstances."

e. Advancement for litigation expenses

RMBCA	DGCL
§8.53 - Advance for Expenses •A corporation may pay for or reimburse the reasonable expenses in advance if: (1) The director affirms good faith belief that he is entitled to indemnification under § **8.51** (2) Director must undertake to repay advancement if it is later determined that he is not entitled to indemnification (no security needed). (3) The other directors or shareholder must know of nothing that would preclude indemnification under §8.55.	**§145(e)** •Expenses including attorney fees may be paid in advance as long as the director undertakes to repay the amount advanced if he is ultimately found not entitled to indemnification.

f. Indemnification of non-directors

RMBCA	DGCL
§8.56 Unless the articles of incorporation provide otherwise: • A corporation may also indemnify officers employees and agents.	**§145 (c)** • No statutory indemnification for officers, employees and agents who are successful on the merits or otherwise in the defense of any action, suit or proceeding to which they are a party by reason of their status (see note infra). This also applies to persons who are no longer directors, officers, employees or agents on or after July 1, 1997.

Note: *Mandatory indemnification* §145(c) of employees and agents under these circumstances continues to be permissible under §145 and, thus *may be granted* by charter, by-law, contract or board resolution, but is no longer mandated by statute with respect to acts or omissions occurring on or after July 1, 1997.

3. Directors & Officers Insurance (D&O)

The corporation can cover its own indemnification liability through insurance. Corporation can buy insurance as compensation for employee.

RMBCA	DGCL
§8.57 - Insurance • This is allowed even if it covers non-indemnifiable expenses because the director could have purchased it herself. Not good for: • improper personal benefit; • bad faith dealing; • illegal compensation; • willful or knowing misconduct; or • a violation of the law.	**§145(g)** • This is allowed even if it covers covering non- indemnifiable expenses. • The director could have purchased it herself. Not good for: • improper personal benefit; • bad faith dealing; • illegal compensation; • willful or knowing misconduct; or • a violation of the law.

J. **The Role of the Shareholders in Running the Corporation**

1. **Shareholder power**

   a. Shareholders are the owners of the corporation, but have a limited role. They have no right to exercise direct management or control over daily (ordinary) corporate affairs.
   b. Shareholders have power to exercise some control through their voting rights.

2. **Shareholder Franchise:**

   - Elect and oust the Board.
   - Amend or replace the by-laws (RMBCA § 10.20).
   - Make non binding recommendations to the board.
   - Inspect records if in good faith, interest, notice and proper purpose.

3. **Shareholders' Meetings**

   a. There are two types of shareholder meetings: called by directors or others authorized in the by-laws (i.e., president or 10% of shareholders).
      - **Annual** - The usual meeting at which directors are elected and regular business matters are performed; and
      - **Special** - called by person authorized in the by-laws for a special purpose which usually is usually by the board, president or a stockholder with a large number of shares.
   b. Shareholders can only act at meetings.
   c. Need quorum to vote.

    d. Corporation must give advanced notice of meetings (usually 10-60 days) which specifies place, date and time. Waiver of notice is allowed.

    e. Need quorum to hold a meeting--usually is an absolute majority of shares entitled to vote.
Some states hold that a meeting can continue even if a shareholder withdraws leaving less than quorum. (*See Duffy v. Loft, Inc.,* 151 A. 223 (Del. 1930); *but see Levisa Oil Corp. v. Quigley,* 234 S.E.2d 257 (Va. 1977) (holding that a meeting cannot continue when majority shareholders withdraw to protect their interests)).

	RMBCA	**DGCL**
Annual Meeting	**§7.01- Annual Meeting** •By-laws will prescribe a fixed date for an annual meeting . •Can be held inside or outside the state as the by-laws direct. If the by-laws are silent then the annual meeting will be held at the corporate headquarters. •Failure to conduct an annual meeting does not effect the validity of corporate action -- general business.	**§211 - Meetings of Stockholders** •§211 (b) The annual meeting must be held on the date and time set by the by-laws; •Any proper business may be transacted at the meeting including election of directors; •§211 (a) The meeting can be held either inside or outside the state as directed in the by-laws. If no place is stated in the by-laws then the meeting will be held in the corporate office; •§211 (c) Failure to hold a meeting shall not effect otherwise valid corporate acts.

f. **Shareholders Minutes**: An *officer* must take minutes of the proceedings of the meetings.

	RMBCA	DGCL
Special Meeting	**§7.02 - Special Meeting** •Can be called by: • the board or person authorized in the articles or by-laws; or •the holder(s) of 10% of the votes by delivering notice to the secretary of the corporation; •May be held inside or outside the state; •Only the business purpose described in the notice under 7.05 may be discussed.	**§211(d)** •Can be called by the board or person authorized by the certificate of incorporation or the by-laws; •Can only discuss the purposes described in the notice under **§222**.

	RMBCA	DGCL
Court Ordered Meeting	**§7.03** •§ A shareholder can apply to the court to order an annual meeting if: • No annual meeting was held within 6 months after the end of the fiscal year; or • 15 months have elapsed since the last meeting. •A shareholder can apply to the court to order a special meeting if: • a special meeting was not held when it was required; or • Notice of a special meeting was not given within 30 days of a shareholder demand for one under §7.02; •A court can fix the time, place, date, quorum and purpose of a meeting it orders.	**§211** (c) •If there is a failure to old an annual meeting for 30 days after the designated date, or if no date has been set, for a period of 13 months after the organization of the corporation or after its last annual meeting, the court may order a meeting upon a shareholder's application. •The court may determine the time, place, record date, quorum and form of the meeting.

	RMBCA	**DGCL**
Action without a Meeting (Consent Solicitation)	**§7.04 - Action without meeting** •Signed unanimous consent by all shareholders is needed for approval of a transaction without a meeting.	**§228 - Consent of Stockholders in Lieu of Meeting** •Any action that may be taken at an annual or special meeting may be taken without a meeting if: • Shareholders send a signed consent -- no prior notice needed. • Notice is sent to all shareholders even those not voting. •Only majority consent is needed (the same as required if there is a meeting).

	RMBCA	DGCL
Notice	**§7.05 Notice of meeting** •Applies to annual and special meetings; •Only needs to be given to shareholders entitled to vote at the meeting. •The board must inform shareholders within 10-60 days before the meeting date. •Notice must include the date, time and place of the meeting. •Notice must include the purpose(s) and description of a special meeting (not required for an annual meeting). •Notice must set a record date (**§7.07**). If it is not set, the record date is 1 day before the first notice is delivered to the shareholders. (**§7.06**).	**§222 - Notice of Meetings** •Written notice must be given whenever stockholders are entitled to take action at a meeting (applies to annual and special meetings). •Notice must be in writing and state place, date, and time of a special or annual meeting. •Notice for a special meeting must include a business purpose. •Notice must be given within 10-60 days before the meeting date. •If the notice is mailed, then it is deemed effective when mailed.
Waiver of Notice	**§7.06** • Shareholders may waive any notice requirement in writing if signed and delivered to the corporation. •Attendance at a meeting waives any objections to notice unless the shareholder objects at the beginning of the meeting.	**§229** •A written, signed waiver of notice is equivalent to actual notice. •Attending a meeting will waive a notice requirement unless the shareholder objects at the beginning of the meeting.

	RMBCA	DGCL
Record Date	**§7.07 Record Date** •The by-laws fix a record date; or •The board may fix a record date. •The date can not be more than 70 days before the meeting or action. **§7.02 For a special meeting** The record date for determining the shareholders entitled to vote is the date the first shareholder signs the demand for a meeting;	**§213 Fixing the date to determine the shareholders of Record** •The *record date* is determined by the board. •It can not be less than 10 or more than 60 days before the meeting and cannot precede the date of the Board resolution fixing the *Record date*. •If no date is chosen, then the record date is the day before notice is sent to the shareholders or the day before the meeting if notice is waived.
Quorum	**§7.25 - Quorum** •Quorum is a majority of voting shares unless the articles of incorporation states otherwise. •At least a majority of the shareholders present must vote for a decision--the board may require a greater quorum. •Once a share is present for one purpose, it is present for all purposes. •To change the quorum or voting numbers the correct amount present to vote is required (§7.27).	**§216 - Quorum and Required Vote for Stock Corporations** •Usually stated in the by-laws. •Cannot be less than one-third of the shares entitled to vote. •If the by-laws are silent, quorum is: • The majority of all shares entitled to vote (in person or through proxy); • In all matters other than election of directors a *majority* of quorum is required to take action; • The election of directors requires a *plurality* of quorum to take action; • If voting by class, quorum is a majority of each class.

4. Voting Rights (*see also Proxy discussion infra*)

    a.   **Shareholders vote on fundamental changes:**
- Sell all or substantially all the assets.
- Certain types of mergers (statutory, share exchange).
- Conflict of interest transactions.
- Amendment of the Certificate of Incorporation.

Most shareholder's in publicly held corporations vote through proxy instead of physical presence at the actual place of the meeting.

A **Proxy** is a shareholder's grant to another to exercise that shareholder's voting rights at the meeting.
- Proxies are used for both director elections and corporate actions.
- Management usually solicits proxies, although individual shareholders can also make proxy solicitations.
- Proxies are completely dependent on full and fair disclosure.
- There is a lot of incentive for Large **Institutional** investors to get involved but very little reason for other investors to get involved.

Individual shareholders generally *do not* get involved for 2 reasons:

    (i) Free Rider Problem-

        Shareholders ask: Others will do it, why me? Little incentive for little shareholders to collectivize their power to reform management. Therefore, they wait for one person to take action. It is very expensive to get the other shareholders' to collectivize for a vote and if the shareholder loses on the issue he absorbs all costs, but if he wins, the benefits get divided by the entire group after he is reimbursed.

(ii) Rational Apathy

If a shareholder has a small stake in the firm, he will rationalize that the time he put into reading the materials on the corporation will not be worth it because he will only receive minimal gain. Therefore, the average individual shareholder does not read the materials and usually votes for or with incumbent directors. Large or institutional shareholders do not have this problem because their stake in the corporation is much higher.

Note: The free rider and rational apathy problems are good for management because management will be able to do what they want. However, if there is an institutional investor, then managers can have a problem because the institutional investors will want more say in the organization and therefore, the corporation.

b. **Only *shareholders of record* can vote** (determined by statute or the by-laws).

A shareholder who sells his stock after the *record date* can still vote (or give the new shareholder a proxy) however, if the new owner is injured by the previous owner's vote, he may be entitled to damages (*See, e.g., In re Grant Portland Cement Co.*, 21 A.2d 697 (Del. 1941)).

c. **Some classes of stock are nonvoting.**

d. **Shareholder voting is usually straight** (1 vote per share) and a plurality or majority of affirmative votes is needed to take action.

- This allows a majority owner to control the board.
- To assure minority shareholders are represented on the Board, some states allow cumulative voting when shareholders vote in board elections.

	RMBCA	DGCL
Voting	**§7.25 -Voting Requirements for Voting Groups** •You need a plurality for all matter.	**§216 - Required Vote for Stock Corporations** •All matters except the election of directors require a *majority* of affirmative votes (in person and through proxy); •Election of directors requires a *plurality* of affirmative votes; •Class votes need the affirmative vote of a majority of the stock for all actions.

Record Date--The date set by the corporation to determine who is a "Record Holder" of shares at a specified date and is thereby entitled to vote at a meeting or deliver a consent.

Absolute Majority-- A majority of the possible votes (1000 total votes, need 501 to approve through an absolute majority).

Simple Majority--majority of present votes (1000 votes, 800 present, need 401 to approve through a simple majority).

Plurality--more votes are cast for the proposal than against it.

Supermajority--requires a larger percentage than a mere majority vote.

e.   **Voting Trusts and Voting Agreements:**

Voting Trust is a formal agreement by which record
title (voting rights) is transferred to a trustee and the term
must be less than or equal to 10 YEARS; it may be
extended for an additional 10 years within 2 years of the
end of the initial term.

Voting Agreement has the same requirements as a
Voting Trust except it is between shareholders instead of
shareholders and a trustee (two or more).

f.   **Dual class voting**

Originally shareholders always had 1 vote per share of
stock; however, under modern statutes, this is not
always the case. The modern statutes allow the Board to
issue shares of classes of stock which have greater or
lesser voting rights (or no voting rights at all).

RMBCA	DGCL
§6.01 Authorized Shares •§6.01 (a) The articles of incorporation can authorize one or more classes of shares; •§6.01 (b) At least one class must have unlimited voting rights. •§6.01 (c) The articles can authorize shares that have special, limited or conditional voting rights. **§6.02 Terms of class or Series determined by the Board** •The board will determine the limitations of any class of stock before issuing them.	**§151 Classes and Series of Stocks; Rights** •§151 (a) The corporation can issue one or more classes of stock--any or all of which can have full, limited or no voting powers--as stated in the certificate of incorporation; •§151 (e) classes can be converted into other classes at the option of the shareholder, the corporation or upon the occurrence of a condition.

Management wants to remove shareholders' voting power so as to prevent takeovers. In order to allow the charter or articles to be amended to change the voting rights, the shareholders must vote. The management will give a *Dividend Sweetener* in order to persuade shareholders to give up their voting rights.

A **dividend sweetener** is an agreement to give additional dividends in exchange for less voting power. Therefore, managers and directors would have high voting power with lower dividends while the other shareholders would have lower voting power with higher dividend.

The SEC attempted to state that changing the articles to allow for higher voting was illegal under Rule 19c-4 of the 1934 Securities and Exchange Act. Therefore, you could only have 1 share = 1 vote, unless you make it different from the beginning. This rule however, was held not to apply to the shareholder's right to change their voting power because the SEC is only allowed to regulate via disclosure, not allocate shareholder power.

Business Roundtable v. SEC., 905 F.2d 406 (D.C. Cir. 1990)
Facts: General Motors wanted to issue a second class of stock that only had one half a vote per share. The commission argued that they could not do this as it violated Rule 19c-4.

Held: The state corporate law, not federal securities law controls the allocation of power among classes of shareholders. The SEC only has the power to ensure that the proxy solicitations contain adequate information and disclosure, not to limit shareholder's choices.
Court held that rule 19c-4 could not be enforced by the SEC. 19c-4 attempts to protect *shareholder suffrage*, which the SEC is allowed to do. However, the SEC in being only allowed to regulate disclosure protect the shareholders by ensuring that they are adequately informed.

- 19c-4 interferes with the shareholders right to reallocate the voting power.
- Shareholders must have full disclosure before voting the changes so they are protected.
- This is an area for state action, not the SEC -- The federal government does not create corporate law, the states do.

5.   Shareholder Proposals

a. Rule 14a-7: Obligations of Registrants to Provide a List of, or Mail Soliciting Material to, Security Holders ("Common Carrier" obligation).
  1) If a shareholder notifies the corporation of his intent to distribute opposing material, the management must either:
     (i) Agree to mail the information provided the shareholder defrays the cost; or
     (ii) Provide shareholder with a list of the record shareholders' names and the addresses.
  2) Management can mail the shareholder's proposal separately or together with the corporation's proxy information.
  3) Management usually prefers to mail it themselves so that they do not have to give out the shareholder list.

b. Rule 14a-8: Proposals of Security Holders
This rule allows a shareholder to propose a resolution without bearing risks because the company pays for the proposal expenses.
- This rule is very often used to propose "corporate   responsibility acts" such as affirmative action or political support.
- It is also used to propose better corporate governance.

The shareholder must notify the corporation of his intentions. The corporation is only required to put the proposal into its proxy if it is proper and *the following statutory requirements* are met:

1) **Eligibility-- 14a-8(a)(1)**
   - The proponent must be a record or beneficial shareholder who owns at least 1% of the voting stock or a $1,000 market value of securities;
   - The proponent must own these securities for at least one year before submitting the proposal; and
   - The proponent must continue to own these securities through the meeting date.

2) **Notice & Attendance-- 14a-8(a)(3)**
   - The proposal must be in resolution form:
   - The proposal must be presented in person at the meeting (or through a representative); and
   - The proposal must include all required information to show that the proponent is eligible.

3) **Time-- 14a-8(a)(3)**
   - Any proposal to be presented at an annual meeting must be received 120 days in advance of the corporation's proxy release in connection with the prior years' annual meeting;
   - If a proposal is to be presented at a special meeting, the corporation must receive notice in a reasonable time.

4) **Number of Proposals**
   - A proponent may submit no more that one proposal.

5) **Supporting Statement**
   - A proposal and its supporting statement may not exceed 500 words;
   - Management can include an opposing statement in its proxy cards;
   - The proxy card must allow shareholders to vote for or against the proposal.

6) **Management may omit a proposal from its proxy for 13 reasons.**

   These 13 reasons generally lead to the exclusion of most proposals:
   a) If the proposal is not proper subject for shareholder action under state laws;
   b) If the proposal would require the registrant to violate any law;
   c) If the proposal is intended to redress a personal claim or to benefit the proponent or to further a personal interest;
   d) If the proposal relates to operations which account for less than 5% of the corporation's total assets at the end of the most recent year;
   e) For less than 5% of its net earnings and gross sales;
   f) If the proposal is not significantly related to the company;
   g) If the proposal is beyond the corporations power;
   h) If the proposal relates to the conduct of the ordinary business operations;
   i) If the proposal relates to an election of officers or directors;
   j) If the proposal counters a proposal submitted by the corporation;
   k) If the proposal duplicates a previously submitted proposal which will be included;

      l)   If the proposal had previously been proposed and rejected within 5 years. If the proposal failed to get 3% on its first try, 6% on its second try, or 10% on its third try; or

      m) If the proposal relates to specific amounts of cash or dividends.

If the management decides to exclude a submitted proposal, it must forward the proposal and its reasons to the S.E.C. for review. The SEC will issue a no-action letter if it agrees with management.

Why are these exclusions allowed?
- Preserves the state law concept that corporate governance should be centralized with management.
- Remove illegal or deceptive proposals.

If management fails to include a proposal that was not properly excluded the shareholder may:
a) Seek under Rule 14a-8(d) an SEC determination that the proxy rules have been violated; or
b) Bring a private action in federal court to enjoin management solicitations or to forcibly include the shareholder's proposal.

Lovenheim v. Iroquois Brands, Inc., 618 F. Supp. 554 (D.C. Cir. 1985)

Facts: A shareholder wanted to include a proposal to prevent the company from treating geese inhumanely in its pate' production.

Held: That while the pate' was not a significant part of the corporation's business, the proposal was *non-excludable* because it *related to* an important *social policy*. Thus, the significance of a proposal is not a purely financial issue.

Note: Public Policy cannot be excluded, even if it is a matter of ordinary business.

6. The role of inspection rights in shareholder proposals

RMBCA	DGCL
§16.02 - Inspection of Records by Shareholders •Entitles a shareholder to inspect and copy, during regular business hours at the corporation's principal office, records described in 16.01(e). Shareholder must give corporation written notice at least 5 business days before he wants to inspect the records; a shareholder refers to both a shareholder of record and a beneficial shareholder. •Shareholders are entitled to inspect and copy Board minutes, accounting records and the record of shareholders only if the following requirements are met: 1. Good faith demand for a proper purpose; 2. Describe with reasonable particularity the purpose of the inspections and the records that are to be inspected; 3. The records requested must be directly connected to the purpose.	**§220 - Stockholder's Right of Inspection** •Only stockholders of **record**, not beneficial stockholders are entitled to inspect records. • A proper purpose is needed and the inspection must be related to the persons interest as a stockholder. •Inspection is only allowed during normal business hours. •The shareholder must make a written demand stating the proper purpose stated. •Shareholders can inspect and copy: Stock ledgers, shareholder lists and other books and records. •The Court of Chancery has exclusive jurisdiction over whether a shareholder is entitled to inspection rights.

RMBCA	DGCL
§16.01(e) Documents the corporation must keep at the corporate headquarters Articles, by-laws, resolutions, shareholder meeting minutes, written communications to shareholders, names and business addresses of all directors and officers, and recent annual report.	

a. Shareholders inspection of records?

1) As a right:
>Articles of Incorporation;
>By-laws;
>Shareholder Meeting Minutes.

2) Available upon showing a *proper purpose*
>Board Minutes;
>Accounting Records;
>Shareholder Lists;
>>Most fights are over releasing the shareholder lists.

b. Proper Purpose

1) Something within the shareholders economic interest as a shareholder (interest in investment in the company).
2) *Not* curiosity or annoyance or a purpose that is hostile to the corporation.
3) The fact that there is also an improper purpose does not deny inspection rights for the primary proper purpose.

(See Central Time Corp. v. Talley Industries, 240
A.2d 755 (Del. 1968).

4) Solicitation of proxies.

5) Interest in determining whether the corporation is
being properly managed.

6) Shareholder litigation--to inform shareholders about
and ask them to join the litigation. *(See Compaq
Computer Corp. v. Horton*, 631 A.2d 1 (Del. 1993)).

7) Determine the corporation's financial condition.

8) Selling the records or stockholder list to a competitor
is **not a proper purpose**.

c. Burden to Prove a Proper Purpose

• At common law, the shareholder had the burden of
proving a proper purpose. (*See, e.g. Albee v. Lamson
& Hubbard Corp.*, 69 N.E.2d 811 (Mass 1946).

• Most courts today hold that under the statutes the
corporation has the burden of proving the shareholder
has an improper purpose unless a statute explicitly
states otherwise. (*See, e.g. Crane Co. v. Anaconda
Co.*, 346 N.E. 2d 507 (NY 1976).

State ex rel. Pillsbury v. Honeywell, Inc., 191
N.W.2d 406 (Minn. 1971)
The plaintiff purchased stocks to gain inspection rights. He
wanted to inspect the stockholder records so that he could
convince shareholders to prescribe to his philosophy (Don't
build weapons), not to help the corporation.
Held: This is not a proper purpose.

Delaware courts *have not* followed this.

See Credit Bureau Reports, inc. v. Credit Bureau of St. Paul, Inc. 290 A.2d 691 (Del. 1972) (holding that solicitation of proxies is reasonably related to a shareholder's interest even if there is a secondary purpose).

7. Shareholder Litigation

a. Why Sue?

Shareholders can bring a direct suit to remedy a breach of a duty owed to them directly.
- Managers owe duties to the shareholders with regard to managing the corporations business.
- Managers owe duties to the shareholders with regard to the exercise of their rights, such as the right to vote.

b. How to Sue

1) Shareholders must first request that the Board of Directors remedy the situation. RMBCA § 7.42.

2) In Delaware, the lack of a demand may be excused if it would be inappropriate.

   (i) There are four reasons why a demand may be inappropriate:
     (1) Futility;
     (2) Exigencies of time;
     (3) Irrelevance; or
     (4) Would lead to a suit which deprives counsel of their fees.

(ii)   The purpose of the requirement of a demand is three fold:
   (1)   Prevents strike suits;
   (2)   Gives directors a chance to take action; and
   (3)   Judicial economy.

RMBCA	DELAWARE
•Suit can be filed if directors reject or do nothing after 90 days.	•Directors must ignore demand to allow for a derivative suit. If the Board does consider it, the Board's decision is subject to the Business Judgment Rule.

After a demand is made:

Derivative suit: Suit, on behalf of the corporation, against a third party, most often concerning careless managers or managers acting in bad faith. A derivative suit is two suits in one:
   (1) suit in equity; and
   (2) suit to enforce corporate rights.

All recovery in derivative suits generally go to the corporation. If victorious shareholder receives attorney's fees.

8.   **Controlling Shareholders**

   a.   **General requirements**
      1)   There is *no fiduciary duty statute for controlling shareholders,* however courts impose a duty upon controlling shareholders because their position gives them the ability to exert pressure on the board.

2) Fiduciary duties will be imposed on a controlling shareholder even if the shareholder is not a director or an officer of the corporation.

3) The controlling shareholder cannot take advantage of his position and use his control premium. He can effect change to prejudice the minority shareholder. But most avoid *Zahn (see infra)* type situations.

4) Controlling shareholders can either be individuals or other corporations or entities who own shares in the corporation.

5) There is no definition as to what percentage of a company an individual must own to have a duty imposed, however some courts have held that as little as 14% was enough. This is a case by case determination. If the votes are very dispersed, then one large concentration will have significant control.

6) The corporate opportunity doctrine also applies to controlling shareholders. (See, A.L.I. Corp. Gov. § 5.12).

7) The controlling shareholders also owe a duty to the minority shareholders when bringing about fundamental changes in the corporation.

8) *See Pepper v. Litton*, 308 U.S. 295 (1939) (holding that a controlling shareholder can not use its control *to exploit or oppress* the minority shareholders).

9) *See also Donahue v. Rodd Electrotype Co.*, 328 N.E.2d 505 (Mass. 1975) (holding that a controlling shareholder will breach his fiduciary duties if he causes the corporation to purchase some of his shares and does not require the corporation to offer the minority shareholders an equal opportunity).

b. **Dealings Between the Controlling Shareholder and the Corporation**

1) The controlling shareholder should not engage in *self dealing.*

2) In dealings between the controlling shareholder and the corporation, the controlling shareholders cannot unfairly benefit at the expense of the minority shareholders.

3) The *Duty of Loyalty* and *Duty of Care* only apply if the minority shareholders can show that there is a *conflict of interest and that the controlling shareholder benefits* when the corporation does not.

The *burden is on the minority shareholder* to show that the majority shareholder has engaged in an arms length transaction.

This differs from the traditional fiduciary test where the fiduciary (director or officer) has the duty to show that their transactions were fair when there is a conflict. However, if the controlling shareholder enters into a transaction with the corporation, the burden of proof is on the controlling shareholder to show that the transaction is fair.

If the controlling shareholder is on the both sides of a transaction and there is an unequal benefit, then intrinsic fairness requires that the Duty of Loyalty applies.

If there is *no unequal benefit,* then the *Business Judgment Rule applies* and protects the controlling shareholder-- shielding him from liability.

Zahn v. Transamerica Corp., 162 F.2d 36 (3d Cir. 1947)

Facts: Transamerica owned nearly all of a particular class of stock in the Axton-Fisher Tobacco company. It exercised its control over the board to redeem all of its class A stock--a class that had no voting rights. After the shares were redeemed, the corporation liquidated and only Transamerica--the controlling shareholder benefited from the liquidation ($240 per share). Another class A shareholder sued claiming that he should have been allowed to benefit from the liquidation.

Held: Transamerica unfairly used its controlling share of the corporation to profit at the expense of the minority shareholders thereby violating its fiduciary duty as a controlling shareholder.

Sinclair Oil v. Levien, 280 A.2d 717 (Del. 1971)

Facts: Sinclair Oil owned 97% of a subsidiary (SV). Sinven paid out very large dividends both to Sinclair oil and its minority shareholders--the dividends did not however exceed the allowed amount under DGCL § 170. The dividends did however exceed Sinven's net earnings. A minority shareholder of Sinven sued Sinclair claiming that the dividends were excessive and that Sinclair breached its duty as a controlling shareholder in paying them out since it received the majority of the benefit (by reason that it was a large shareholder). The minority shareholder also claimed that Sinclair usurped corporate opportunity by stealing business form Sinven through its control as the majority shareholder. It also claimed that Sinclair forced Sinven to enter into contracts with a wholly owned subsidiary. Such contracts required fixed high quantity purchases and full payment on receipt.

Held:

1. This is not a breach of the duty of loyalty because the minority received their appropriate share--the controlling shareholder did not benefit at the minority's expense. Thus, *no preference or additional benefit was given to the controlling shareholder to the exclusion of the minority shareholders.*

Note: However, the *intrinsic fairness test will apply* if the partially owned subsidiary had a contract with the wholly owned subsidiary and if the wholly owned subsidiary breached the contract and the parent never directed the partially owned to sue for the breach. Here, the wholly owned would have a benefit to the exclusion of the partially owned. This results in a breach of the Duty of Loyalty of the controlling shareholder.
The opportunities that Sinclair used exclusively for itself were not corporate opportunities. There was no evidence that Sinven had any unique abilities to develop the opportunities thus requiring them to be turned over. Nothing came directly to Sinven. Therefore, there is no benefit that Sinclair received to the exclusion of the minority.

c. **A.L.I. § 5.10**

1. A controlling shareholder who enters into a transaction with the corporation and fulfills his duty of fair dealing to the corporation if:
   a) The transaction is *reasonable and fair* to the corporation *at the time the corporation enters* into it; and,
   b) The *disinterested shareholders authorize or ratify the transaction in advance* after complete disclosure about the

conflict of interest as long as the transaction will not waste the corporation's assets.

2. If this is done, the burden of proof is on the person challenging the transaction. If these steps are not followed, then the burden of proof is on the controlling shareholder. If the transaction is done in the ordinary course of business, then the burden of proof is on the person challenging the transaction.

d. **Duties of controlling shareholders in change of control situations**

Jones v. Ahmanson, 1 Cal. 3d 93 (1969)
Facts: The majority shareholders of a "United Savings and Loan Association," whose shares were sold at a very high price on the market, set up a holding company and transferred its shares to that company. The majority shareholder then sold the shares to the holding company on the public market. This enabled persons who would otherwise not be able to buy shares of "United" to now do so. It also a allowed the majority shareholders to cash out on their investment more easily because it could sell shares of the holding company at a lower price than "United" shares. Unfortunately, it also impeded the minority shareholders' ability to sell its "United" shares. The minority shareholders sued the majority shareholders for a breach of fiduciary duty.

Held: The majority shareholder breached their fiduciary duties. His actions had no legitimate business justification and the majority shareholders did not give the minority shareholders the opportunity to participate in the

133

transaction. Controlling shareholders may not use their power to benefit themselves to the detriment of the minority, they owe a duty of "good faith and inherent fairness . . . in any transaction in which control of the corporation is material."

e. Squeeze Out or Cash Out Mergers

A *cash out merger* is when the majority owner acquires all of the shares in the target corporation by exchanging shares of the minority shareholders with or without their approval.

This usually occurs when a parent corporation merges a majority owned subsidiary into either itself or a wholly owned subsidiary. The majority shareholder *squeezes out* the minority shareholders by exchanging the shares of the target corporation for cash or other consideration.

There is a *clear conflict of interest* when the majority will want to pay the minority the least for his shares. Additionally, the majority will have more control over the merger terms and therefore will be in a position to take advantage of the minority shareholders. Some states do not require that the shareholders satisfy the fiduciary duties when a squeeze out merger occurs. Delaware and many states provide that the controlling shareholders must use the fair price and fair dealing standards when conducting a squeeze out merger. (*See e.g., Alpert v. 28 William Street Corp.*, 473 N.E.2d 19 (N.Y. 1984); *Weinberger v. UOP, Inc.*, 457 A.2d 701 (Del. Super. Ct. 1983) (discussed *infra*).

1) **Business Purpose Test**

Some courts requires that a controlling shareholder show that there was *a proper business purpose* for the cash out merger. The business purpose must show that the "squeezed out" corporation is benefited by the merger. (*See Coggins v. New England Patriots Football Club*, 492 N.E.2d 1112 (Mass. 1986) (holding that if the purpose for the squeeze out merger was to aid the controlling shareholder in paying back a personal debt, the business purpose test was not satisfied)); *See also Alpert v. 28 William St. Corp.*, 473 N.E.2d 19 (N.Y. 1984) (holding that the business purpose test was met because the merger allowed the squeezed out corporation to attract new capital investors).

Delaware previously required that controlling shareholders satisfy the business purpose test. (*See Singer v. Magnavox Co.*, 380 A.2d 969 (Del. 1977). This requirement was removed in *Weinberger v. UOP*, Inc., 457 A.2d 701 (Del. Super. Ct. 1983) (discussed *infra*). Thus today, Delaware gives no protection to minority shareholders beyond:

- Intrinsic fairness; and
- Expanded appraisal rights under DGCL § 262.

2) Requirement of a **Fair Deal and Fair Price**

Due to the inherent fear that a controlling shareholder will use its power to the minority shareholder's detriment, there must be both a fair price and fair dealing in all squeeze out mergers.

Rosenblatt v. Getty Oil Co., 493 A.2d 929 (Del. Super. Ct. 1985)

Facts: Getty merged with its majority owned subsidiary, Skelly Oil Co. through a squeeze out merger. The merger was negotiated by Skelly's independent-outside directors, there were heated negotiations and both Getty and Skelly retained independent outside investment bankers to advise them and evaluate fair prices.

Held: The court shifted the burden of proof from Getty (the Skelly controlling shareholder) to Skelly's minority shareholders and found that Getty sufficiently satisfied its fiduciary duties to the minority shareholders of Skelly. The merger terms including the price per share were not dictated by Getty and the minority shareholders were fully informed of all material facts relating to the merger.

Weinberger v. UOP, Inc. 457 A.2d 701 (Del. Super. 1983)

Facts: Signal Corporation, the majority shareholder of "UOP," attempted a squeeze out merger between the two companies. The merger negotiations were organized by a person who was a director of both companies. This director did not question the terms of the merger which were proposed by Signal. Signal imposed a short time period to analyze the deal that did not allow the outside investment bank to adequately evaluate UOP's net worth. An internal report prepared by persons who were directors of both companies revealed that any price up to $24 was a fair price for the merger. However, this report was not shown to the independent outside directors of either company and the merger price was only $21.

Held: Signal breached its duty of fair dealing and fair price because the material facts were not disclosed and the minority shareholders were not fully informed. In coming to this decision, the court created a two part entire fairness test to determine whether a merger was fair.

3) **Entire Fairness Test - Two Part**:

   a) **Fair Price**

   To value the corporation - look at all factors including: the discounted cash flow; *fair value* of the assets minus the liabilities; the past and future prospective earnings; the market value of both companies; profits or money saved from the merger; and the net book value of each company.

   Any financial valuation method accepted by the financial community can be utilized to determine a fair price.

   b) **Fair Dealings**

      (i) The transaction should allow sufficient time for independent advisors to examine each corporation: when the transaction is timed, how it is to be initiated, etc.

      (ii) The approval of the minority shareholders must have been obtained through complete and fair disclosure.

      (iii) The Board of the parent corporation (the majority shareholder) must disclose all relevant information and reports prepared by directors or officers.

      (iv) The Boards should set up a special negotiating committee, comprised of independent outside directors, to ensure an arms length transaction.

In *Weinberger,* the test failed because:

   (i) There was a corporate report stating that the fair price would be higher than they actually received which was not disclosed;

   (ii) Rushed method of achieving the fairness report;

   (iii) There was no price negotiation; and,

(iv) Neither the minority shareholders nor the Boards were completely informed.

Delaware Block Method of valuation: The court separately determines the value of a corporation's stock under different basis of valuation (usually market value, asset value and dividend value) and then assigns a weight to each valuation. The value of the stock is then valued as the weighted average of all the valuations.

4) **The Burden of Proof**
The majority or controlling shareholders have the burden of proof to show that the deal is fair. If they have completely disclose all material facts, the burden will switch to the minority shareholders to show that the deal is unfair.

5) **Remedies for unfair cash out mergers**

- If a court finds a violation of the controlling shareholder's duty of fair dealing, it will usually try to stop or rescind the merger. *(See Rabkin v. Phillip A. Hunt Chemical Corp.*, 498 A.2d 1099 (Del. Supr. Ct. 1985).
- If, however, this is not possible the court *can award appraisal rights or rescissionary* damages.

    - *Appraisal rights* will give the shareholders the market price on the date of the merger.
        If there is deliberate misrepresentation, such as fraud or self dealing, then there may be more damages other than appraisal (*See* RMBCA § 13.02).
    - *Rescissionary damages* will put the shareholders in the same economic position that they would have been in had the merger not occurred--this usually means the current market value of the stock.

138

K. Corporate Authorities

1. Agency relationships

The power to transact business for the corporation.

  a. **Express Authority** - specifically given - such as
     Board passes a resolution, statute, articles of
     incorporation, and by-laws.

  b. **Implied Actual Authority** - actually based on past
     actions (i.e., internal appearance, officer buys
     equipment)
     - *Test*: You imply such power because of a previous
       purchase and Board didn't complain, plus you have
       the corporate position.
     - This binds the corporation.

  c. **Apparent Authority** - (i.e., External appearance;
     foreman is told not to buy without permission. One day
     he buys without permission.)
     - *Test*: Is it reasonable for a seller to assume that a
       foreman would have such authority?

  d. **Ratification** (i.e., Foreman buys a truck; boss says
     don't do it again). Unauthorized action of agent is
     approved but no authority in the future.

2. How to determine who has the authority to bind the corporation

When dealing with a subsidiary that wishes a parent to guarantee the loan, it is important to prove that the people at the parent corporation have the appropriate authority.

a. Ascertain the fact that Parent and Subsidiary are both legal entities:
   - Look at charters and certificates filed with the Secretary of State.
   - Make sure that they have paid taxes and are in good standing.

b. Ascertain that they have the power to act, to enter into such a contract:
   - Look at the statute and the charter.
   Make sure that the Board has approved and authorized the transaction.
   - Look at the minutes and resolutions.

c. Ascertain that you are dealing with the right person:
   - Do they have authority from the Board?
   - Are they whom they say they are?

Quo Warranto is a common law writ used to test whether the person exercising the power is legally entitled to do so.

V. LIMITATIONS ON LIMITED LIABILITY

A. Introduction

One of the chief advantages of the corporate form is limited liability. However, this limited liability "veil" can be "pierced" if there are instances of abuse.

- In general, shareholders are not liable beyond their investment in the corporation. The corporation separates the risk of doing business from its investors and managers.

- **"Piercing the Corporate Veil"**-- is a way that the shareholders are held personally liable to the corporation's creditors.

Under RMBCA §6.22 & DGCL §102(b)(6), the shareholder is not liable for the debts of the corporation:
- The shareholders are only required to pay the consideration that is owed for the purchase of the stock.
- This encourages capital formation and investment and helps small enterprises develop.
- Liability is limited to the shareholder's investment, and therefore is less risky.
- Shareholders cannot use the corporation as a shield. There is a limited amount of protection and if it is abused, then the veil of non-liability will be pierced.

B. Dissolution and Liquidation

1. **Dissolution**: *The end of the corporation's legal existence.* Its termination can occur in any manner, whether by expiration of charter, decree of court, act of legislature, *or by Board resolution:*
   (i) Shareholder meeting to take action upon resolution;
   (ii) Shareholder vote;
   (iii) No need for director action; dissolution can be authorized if all shareholders consent in writing and the certificate of dissolution is filed with the secretary of state.

   After the filing of a certificate of dissolution with the Secretary of State, the corporation is technically dissolved but the powers of the corporation and its directors continue to finish the affairs of the corporation.
   The right to dissolve a corporation without its consent belongs entirely to the state.

   a. **Voluntary Dissolution** occurs where the proposal to dissolve is initiated by the Board and usually requires approval by a majority of voting shares.

   b. **Involuntary Dissolution** occurs upon the granting of a petition presented to the court by a specified percentage of shareholders, on grounds which have been defined by statute.

   c. *De Facto* **Dissolution** occurs when a corporation suspends all its operations due to insolvency or other reasons, and goes into *liquidation* without availing itself of the statutory procedure provided for that purpose. A dissolution by any other means is a dissolution by law.

2. Liquidation: Assemble all the corporation's assets, settle with the creditors and debtors, and apportion the remaining assets, if any, among the stockholders.

C. Agency Instrumentality Theory

1) Courts are willing to pierce the corporate veil *if corporate formalities are not kept*, that is:
   (i) No separate entity is maintained; and
   (ii) The corporation is the instrumentality (alter ego) of the shareholders.

In dealing with a parent-subsidiary situation if corporate formalities are not kept the court will pierce the veil. If the managers, employees, officers, board, accountants, etc., of the parent and subsidiary are the same (the court will look at the various factors) the courts may pierce the veil.. However, if the corporate formalities are kept, then the courts will not pierce the veil.

- **"Dummy" corporation** - This occurs when a corporation is being used to generate income which is then drained off. There is nothing wrong with forming a dummy corporation to limit liability as long as the formalities are maintained. Thus, absent any other grounds, courts will not Pierce the Corporate Veil.

- If a creditor knows that he is dealing with a dummy corporation, then the creditor will be liable for its contracts with the corporation. However, courts are generally willing to *pierce the veil for fraud.*

D. **Grounds for Piercing the Corporate Veil**

1. **Undercapitalization** - Creditor must show that the corporation did not have enough funds for the foreseeable business needs and that he (the creditor) had no way of knowing will very often pierce the corporate veil.

2. **Failure to follow corporate formalities** - No annual meetings, no issued shares--nothing that shows that the corporation is acting as a separate, independent corporation. This will very often pierce the corporate veil.
   - This is also true for *commingling* assets and affairs or sharing managers, since doing so can confuse the creditor about whom they are dealing.

3. **Involuntary creditors** - In situations where the creditor can't protect himself via contracts (i.e., torts), the court may pierce the veil more often than voluntary situations, such as employees, suppliers, et. al., where the parties contract into a situation and can protect themselves.

4. **Commingling assets**--If an individual shareholder's assets are commingled with the corporations assets, courts will very often pierce the corporate veil. If an individual or other corporation owns most of the stock of the corporation and controls or dominates the corporate policies, then the veil may be pierced for that shareholder only.

5. **Misrepresentation** - if a shareholder or manager creates the misrepresentation that business is in good condition when in fact it is not, courts are more willing to pierce the corporate veil. Courts are generally willing to pierce for *fraud.*

Note: All the grounds above, piercing the corporate veil only applies to those shareholders who actively participated in the corporate action. For instance, if the court pierces the veil to hold a fraudulent shareholder liable only that shareholder may be sued not all shareholders.

Walkovszky v. Carlton, 223 N.Y.2d 414 (1966)
Facts: Walkovszky was run over by a cab and sued Carlton, a stockholder of the cab company. Carlton owned 10 cab companies, each was under insured, undercapitalized and owned only two cabs.

Held: The veil will not be pierced. I Inadequate capitalization alone will not lead to liability absent a finding that the corporation abused the arrangement by failing to *follow corporate formalities*, there is no personal liability.

Minton v. Cavaney, 364 P.2d 473 (Cal. App. Dep't. Supr. Ct. 1961).
Facts: Plaintiff's daughter died in a pool owned by the corporation. The plaintiff procured a judgment against the corporation, but the corporation had inadequate capital. The defendant, a director-officer-shareholder of the corporation, stated that the corporation never functioned as a corporation.

Held: The director is liable because he was an active participant of an undercapitalized corporation that failed to follow formalities.

Bartle v. Home Owners Cooperative, 309 N.Y. 103 (1955)
Facts: Defendant corporation was the sole shareholder of a subsidiary corporation. All corporate formalities were maintained, no misleading statements were made to creditors and the defendant did not deplete the corporations assets. The subsidiary corporation was sold and later became bankrupt. Creditors sued the parent corporation.

Held: The defendant Corporation was not liable. The defendant corporation did not act fraudulently or illegally and made no misrepresentations.

The outcome would have been different if the corporation acted as a mere shell (*See, e.g. Stone v. Eacho*, 127 F.2d 284 (4th Cir. 1942)).

Brunswick Corporation v. Waxman, 599 F.2d 34

In a contract situation there is no basis for piercing the veil of a corporation that is known to have no assets and is a "Dummy" corporation, absent fraud or misrepresentations. In such a situation, there must be an involuntary act to entitle the plaintiff to pierce the veil

This is because without fraud or misrepresentations, there is no wrongdoing; and if one does not protect himself, why should the court?

Kinney Shoe Corporation v. Polan, 939 F.2d 209

The plaintiff wanted to hold the defendant, the sole owner of a corporation liable on a lease. The corporation had no assets and was a mere shell corporation.

Held: The shareholder is liable. If no formalities are followed, there is no capital contribution, and the defendant deliberately uses the corporation as a shield from liability, then the veil will be pierced.

E. Deep Rock Doctrine
 (*Equitable Subordination* of a shareholder's claims)

- If the corporation becomes insolvent, the claims of a
  controlling shareholder, who is also a creditor of the
  corporation, may be subordinated to (or ranked below) the
  claims of other creditors if the controlling shareholder engages
  in certain actions including, but not limited to:
    - Fraud;
    - Undercapitalization;
    - Grossly negligent mismanagement;
    - Commingling of funds;
    - Failure to observe corporate formalities.

See, e.g., Taylor v. Standard Gas & Electric Co., 306
U.S. 307 (1939). Codified in the Bankruptcy Code.

VI. PROXY VOTING: State and Federal Regulation

A. Introduction:

Proxy voting is often the machinery through which many corporate activities are done, i.e., election/removal of directors, shareholder proposals, etc.

1. Annual meeting
The meeting date and record date are set by the Board.

2. Shareholder Voting
The proxy is not an official ballot--it is a power of attorney. The shareholders give instructions to the proxy on how they vote in a particular situation. The Board selects who will hold the proxies.

3. Control of the Machinery
The corporation bears the expense of the proxy solicitation and record keeping. If a shareholder wishes to duplicate this, then he must bear the expense.

B. State Regulation

1. Proxy Revocability
   a. Statutes limit the effective period of the proxies.

   b. Shareholder's can usually revoke a proxy by:
   - Notifying the proxy holder.
   - Giving the proxy to someone else.
   - Attending the shareholder's meeting and either revoking the proxy or voting.
   Note: Merely attending a meeting will not revoke a proxy.

149

    c. A shareholder's death or incapacity does not revoke a proxy unless the corporation is notified in writing.

    d. A proxy can be deemed irrevocable if it explicitly states that it is irrevocable and is "coupled with interest." The interest can be an interest in shares, a person who agreed to purchase the shares or a creditor of the shareholder.

2.   Truthfulness

State law prohibits false or misleading statements in a proxy or any other communication from the management. (*See Lynch v. Vickers Energy Corp.*, 383 A.2d 278 (Del. 1977) (requiring that management be completely candid and imposing liability if the false or misleading information would be considered important by a reasonable shareholder in deciding how to vote).

3.   Counting the Proxy
- The votes are only counted if the proxy holders are contested.
- Proxies can be later revoked by showing up or by granting a proxy to a third party at a later time.
- DGCL § 231 requires an inspector to attest to the validity and number of proxies.
- DGCL § 212 allows telegram and telecopied proxies.

RMBCA	DGCL

§7.22 Proxies
•Must have a signed appointment form.
•Proxies are valid for 11 months, unless longer period is expressed.
•A proxy is revocable by the shareholder unless it explicitly states that it is irrevocable and is coupled with an interest. Irrevocability ends when the interest disappears.
•A shareholder's death or incapacity does not affect a proxy unless notice is given before the proxy is exercised.
	§212 Voting Rights of Stockholders; Proxies; Limitations
	•Shareholder's are entitled to one vote for each share unless the certificate of incorporation states otherwise.
	•A shareholder can authorize another person as a proxy by:
	  • Executing a writing (this can be done by the stockholder or an agent. Fax signatures are sufficient); or
	  • Transmitting the proxy through electronic means (such as telegram or cablegram);
	•A proxy is valid for 3 years, unless longer period is expressed on the proxy.
	•Any copy, fax or other reproduction of the writing may be substituted for the original for all purposes as long as it is complete.
	•A proxy is irrevocable if it states so and is coupled with an interest. The interest can be in the stock itself or the corporation in general.

C.   Federal Regulation - SEC Rules

1.   Generally

Inadequacy of State Regulation led to federal regulation 14(a) (federal proxy rules) of the Securities Exchange Act of 1934. State law recently improving, prohibits false or misleading statements in a proxy or any other communication from the management, (*see Lynch v. Vickers Energy Corp.*, 383 A2d. 278 (Del 1977).

Federal rules protect shareholders from manipulation during the proxy procedure through **fair and adequate disclosure**.

- SEC Rule 14a (1934 Act) is intended to prevent corporate management from taking advantage of the shareholders and harming dissenting shareholders.
- 14(a) applies to *any* proxy solicitation -- whether oral or written -- for any corporation registered under the 1934 Act.

2.   Proxy Solicitations

The SEC has adopted proxy rules which regulate the solicitation of proxies, i.e., "sunshine is the best disinfectant."

a. Rule 14a-1: Definitions
14a-1 (f) **- Proxy** - any action that gives or withholds authority concerning issues which shareholders may decide.
14a-1 (g) - **Proxy statement** - required by Rule 14a-(3)(a) must contain information to the shareholders in connection with a solicitation of proxies.
14a-1 (l) - **Solicitation** - very important because the rules only apply if there is actually a proxy solicitation.
- Any request for a proxy with or without a form.

- Any request to execute, or not to execute or revoke a proxy.
- Furnishing a proxy form to security holders (shareholders) under any circumstances is *reasonably calculated to result in proxy procurement, withholding or revocation.*

Two question analysis to determine if "reasonably calculated":
1. Is the communication addressed to shareholders or the general public?
2. Does the communication try to persuade shareholders to vote a certain way?

- An act that might not otherwise be considered a solicitation is a solicitation if it is part of a *continuous plan* that will culminate in a solicitation of *proxies (See Studebaker Corp. v. Gittlin*, 360 F.2d 692 (2d Cir. 1966) (holding that a letter sent by a shareholder asking other shareholders to authorize an inspection of the shareholder list constituted a proxy solicitation because it was part of a continuous plan*)); see also SEC v. Okin*, 132 F.2d 784, 786 (2d Cir. 1943).

  Note: Today this case would have a different outcome because under 14a-2(b) shareholders can communicate as long as no proxy is asked for or furnished. However, the general rule remains valid for other groups.

b.   Exceptions (not solicitations):
- Furnishing a form to a shareholder based on an unsolicited request.
- A public statement by a shareholder of how he intends to vote. (14a-1(1)(2)).
- Any announcement or communication that neither seeks to act as a proxy nor requests a proxy card.

c. **Rule 14a-2(a)(6) - Exemptions from the rules** (They are solicitations but are not subject to the proxy rules):

- If a company or other person through a public forum *(e.g.,* newspaper) *informs* shareholders of a pending proxy solicitation, identifies proposals covered by the solicitation and indicates where shareholders may obtain statements and forms, then this is exempted from the rules. *(But see, Long Island Lighting Company v. Barbash,* 779 F.2d 793 (2d Cir. 1985) (holding that a communication from a public interest group through a newspaper advertisement was an indirect solicitation because it was reasonably calculated to influence the shareholder's vote.

  Note that the dissent claimed that this rule would make every communication a solicitation even it makes no mention of a proxy)).

Rule 14a-2(a)(1) - If there is communication by brokers to beneficial owners seeking instructions on how to vote, then this is exempted from the rules.

Rule 14a-2(a)(2) - If beneficial owners request from brokers, proxy cards and other information regarding the shares, then this is exempted from rules.

Rule 14a-2(b): Solicitations that do not need to follow filing, disclosure & distribution rules.
In general, if you are not seeking power to act as a proxy, then the rules do not apply unless you are: managers, directors, nominees or those involved in a control fight with management.
- Thus, this rule makes it easier for shareholders to communicate with each other as we would with institutional investors who may be better informed.

- This rule (14a-2(b)) also allows public interest groups that are not acting with or for management, directors (or some other party seeking control) to communicate with shareholders as long as such group does not seek a proxy or request a proxy card.

Safe Harbor Rule 14a-2(b)(1) Shareholders who are not seeking proxy authority and have no substantial (material) interest in the solicitation except for their interest as shareholders are exempt from the rules.

Rule 14a-2(b)(2) Non-management solicitations to less than 10 shareholders.

Rule 14a-2(b)(3) Advice by financial advisors in the ordinary course of business as long as they disclose any interest in the proxy contest and receive no fees from a third party.

3. Filing Proxy Materials
The proxy statements are prepared and filed with the SEC, who may review and comment on the proxy statements. Once the SEC comments are cleared, the proxy statement is delivered to the shareholders.

4. Identifying Shareholders
Since the beneficial owners are usually unknown to the corporation, it is usually done through the record owners. (*see* SEC Rules 14a-13, 14b-1, 14b-2). The beneficial owner gives instructions to the record owner or the record owner can choose how to vote.

5. Mandatory Disclosures

Rule 14a-3(a): Information to be Furnished to Security Holders;

Proxy Statement Requirements:
a. From management (Board)
- Information about the corporation, nominees to the Board, management compensation, conflicts of interest and other matters being voted upon.
- The shareholders must be provided with a copy of the *annual report* either before or simultaneously with a proxy solicitation from the management for the annual meeting. (Rule 14a-3(b)).
- This ensures flow of information between the management and shareholder.

b. From non management (dissident shareholders or an outside group)
- The shareholder must be provided with information about the proxy solicitor as well information about the matter of the proxy.

6. Form of the Proxy

a. Rule 14a-4: Requirements as to the Proxy

A proxy form (card) must specifically state:
1. Who is soliciting;
2. Matters to be acted on at the meeting;.
3. Leave a space for the date;

4.   Allow the shareholder to vote either for, against or
     abstain on the proposal and to vote for a nominee to the
     Board or to withhold authority to vote for a nominee;
5.   The card must explicitly state how the shareholder intends
     to vote;
6.   The solicitation materials must identify all participants in
     a proxy contest;
7.   The compensation of the CEO and the 4 highest paid
     executive officers must be disclosed.

7.   Filing & Distribution

a.   Rule 14a-6: Material Required to be Filed

1.   Preliminary copies of all materials must be filed with the
     SEC at least 10 days before sending them out to the
     shareholders.
     •   This does not apply to annual meetings if the only
         actions are director elections and shareholder
         proposals. (See Rule 14a-8 discussed *infra*).
2.   Final copies of the solicitation materials must be filed
     with the SEC on or before the date they are sent to the
     shareholders.
3.   If the solicitation will be done orally through the
     telephone or in person, copies of the written materials
     used in the process must be filed on or before the day that
     the oral solicitation begins.

8.   Antifraud Provisions

a.   Rule 14a-9: False or Misleading Statements

•   A solicitor cannot submit any false or misleading
    material facts.
•   A solicitor cannot omit *material facts* which make the
    statements false or misleading.

- All material information about which the shareholders are to vote must be fully disclosed. However, the management is not required to show the negatives of a material fact as long as it is fully disclosed. (*See, e.g., Golub v. PPD Corp.*, 576 F.2d 759 (8th Cir. 1978) (holding that a proxy statement disclosing that the managers would receive bonuses during a transaction but not disclosing that the managers might be benefiting themselves at the shareholder's expense did not violate Rule 14-a)).
- A proxy solicitation must accurately reflect all issues -- *see* shareholder proposal rule discussed *infra.*
- As long as a proxy discloses all material facts, it will not violate the Federal Proxy rules even if management's actions breach their fiduciary duties. This is a problem that must be resolved by state law.
- The SEC examination does not ensure that the statements are accurate.
- There is an implied private cause of action based upon tort of deceit.

b.   Definition of Material Facts
The Supreme Court has defined material facts in numerous cases. Generally, a material fact is a fact in which there is substantial likelihood that a reasonable investor would find it important in making an investment decision.

TSC Industries, Inc. v. Northway, Inc., 426 U.S. 438 (1976) The Court held that a corporation's failure to disclose to its shareholders that the company which was buying all of its assets had the same executive officers, owned more than a third of its stock, and was exercising control over the corporation in the sale was a material omission of fact.

Basic Inc., v. Levinson, 485 U.S. 224 (1988)
Held: That the materiality of a fact depends on the balancing of two factors:
1. The probability that an event will occur.
2. The likely magnitude of the event.
If one is high but the other is low the fact may still be material.

    c. Scienter - Is necessary at common law but not in a 14a-9 litigation.

9. **Rule 14a-10: Prohibition of Certain Solicitations**
- No postdated or undated proxies are allowed.
- No proxies that state they will be dated later than the date in which they are actually signed.

D.   Challenging Proxy Fraud via Private Actions

1.   State fraud regulations

Under state law all losses must be related to misrepresentations for shareholders to seek damages for problems with a proxy contest.
- Can only be utilized for misrepresentations.
- The shareholders must show that management knew of the misrepresentation and intended shareholder reliance.
- Shareholders must show that they actually relied on the misrepresentations.

2.   Federal Proxy antifraud

a.   Generally

This is not explicitly mentioned in Rule 14a-9, however, the Supreme Court gave an implied right to challenge a corporate transaction approved by the shareholders through a proxy solicitation that violated the rule. *See J.I. Case v. Borak*, 377 U.S. 426 (1964). Under *Borak*, the shareholders can either sue individually or through a derivative suit. A derivative suit requires a showing of loss to the corporation and an individual suit requires a showing of personal economic loss.

b.   Requirements for a private action - Materiality of the omission or misstatement -- *See supra.*

Management's fault:
Courts are split as to whether the management's <u>omissions</u> must be knowing or if they can be held liable for mere negligence.

Causational link:

When a shareholder brings a suit against management claiming that a proxy contains materially false or misleading information, he does not need to prove that he relied on that information in his vote. *(See Mills v. Electric Auto-Lite Co.*, 396 U.S. 374 (1920).

Generally the Shareholders must show that the misleading proxy materials were an *"essential link"* in obtaining shareholder proxies for a specific transaction and that the transaction was the direct cause of his injury. *(See General Electric v. Cathcart*, 980 F.2d 927 (3d Cir. 1992) (dismissing a shareholders action for damages because the act sued upon--election of directors--did not directly cause the shareholders damage, rather the directors acts after being elected caused the damages).

VII. CHANGE OF CONTROL

A. Duties of the Board in the Change of Control Situation

Duties of the board arise when the board is presented with a bid for control of the corporation that they wish to refuse. The question then becomes what is a legitimate ground for refusal.

1. Long-term v. short-term profits;
2. In process of pursuing more lucrative combination (Time-Warner *see infra*);
3. Other constituency statutes - allow directors to consider the effect of plant closings and other similar considerations which are not solely motivated by profit;
4. Sale to looters;
5. Appropriation of an offer to the corporation or the shareholders; or
6. Who keeps the control premium?

The defenses to a hostile takeover may trigger breaches of fiduciary duties for both the directors and the managers. In the 1980's and early 1990's, a series of Delaware cases began to lay out rules for the fiduciary duties in hostile takeovers.

1. Enhanced scrutiny

UNOCAL v. Mesa Petroleum Co., 493 A.2d 946 (Del. 1985)
Statistics of the takeover:
- A front loaded, hostile, two tiered tender offer for 37% of UNICAL.
- There was junk bond financing in second tier (back end)--thus the offer was very coercive to shareholders.

- A known corporate destroyer (frequent green mailer) financed the tender offer.

Basis of suit: The bidder sued to enjoin the self tender claiming that it was a breach of the director's fiduciary duty.

Director Defenses:
a) Consulting with lawyers and outside investment bankers.
b) Self tender offer by the Board at a premium price that was not available for the shares owned by the bidder (Mesa).

Held: There was no breach of the director's fiduciary duty. The board acted in the shareholder's best interest. Only a majority of outside independent directors acted, and they did not stop the tender offer, they merely attempted to remove the coerciveness.

Rule of Law
All Board defensive actions are subject to *enhanced scrutiny* because of the "omnipresent specter" that the Board is acting in its own best interest. This enhanced scrutiny requires that directors show they had *"reasonable grounds for believing a danger to the corporate policy and effectiveness"* existed.

Note: Directors can't act solely to perpetuate themselves in office.

Defensive mechanisms may only be used as a method to thwart off a takeover attempt *if motivated by a good faith concern for the corporation's welfare free from fraud or misconduct.*

How the courts have defined the Unocal "Enhanced Scrutiny" Intermediate Test - Proportionality:
   a)   The Board must perceive the bidders action as a threat to corporate policy.
   b)   Must show that the Board's action is *proportional* to that threat.

Eliminates presumption that defense tactics are NOT motivated by entrenchment.
   The Board will only uphold defense tactics that are reasonably tied to the shareholders' welfare.

Highest concern is to the shareholder's welfare:
   a)   No longer protecting the corporate enterprise to justify any defense tactic. The defense must be proportional.
   b)   Interests of constituents, employees, creditors etc. are secondary to the shareholder's interest.

The threat is anything inconsistent with shareholder welfare:
   a.   Reaction to a coercive bid.
   b.   Reaction to an underpriced bid.
   c.   Reaction to a bidder who wishes to bust up the corporation if this is not good for the shareholders.

Reaction must be proportional to the threat:
   a.   From an objective standpoint.
   b.   More stringent measures for coercive bids than non coercive bids.
   d.   Neutral reaction to a fair bid if non coercive.

The Board must seek the best value for the Shareholder:
   a.   Auction to multiple bidders.
   b.   Can't prefer one bidder over the other.
   c.   Maximize shareholder value when considering fairness.

2. Fiduciary duties of the Board in hostile takeover situations

Moran v. Household International, Inc., 500 A.2d 1346 (Del. 1985)

Facts: While attempting to thwart a hostile takeover the director's of Household amended its charter to adopt a poison pill. The pill allocated stock option rights to common stock shareholders once a tender offer for 30% of the stock was announced or once a single entity obtained 20% of the stock. Moran, a shareholder, claimed that this was a violation of the director's fiduciary duties and beyond their power.

Held: This was not a violation of the fiduciary duties because a board may protect the corporation from coercive hostile takeovers under the Business Judgment Rule.

Rule: Here the directors had the best interests of the corporation in mind. The board was properly concerned with the coercive nature of front end loaded tender offers and the threat of bust ups of this tender offer, thus, it was a reasonable method to prevent the threat of a takeover.

- The Moran court left open the question of how a poison pill should be used in a take over situation. Additionally, the court failed to answer the question as to if the corporation could keep the pill in place when there was no longer a threat. *See Unitron, Inc. v. American General, Corp.*, 651 A.2d 1361 (Del. 1995).

3.   **Limitations on the Sale of Control**

General Issue: If a shareholder is selling control of the corporation, he has a fiduciary obligation to the minority shareholders in the transaction.

a. **Control Premium:** The difference between the value of the shares in their individual capacity and the value of the shares when you are buying a large block in order to obtain control.

The control premium is the price of control of the corporation, that is, the price paid over market price for the controlling shares.

- As a general rule, a controlling shareholder has the right to sell his stock at a premium and to keep the premium as long as the controlling shares were not sold to looters and the sale does not violate the controlling shareholders duty of loyalty. This ensures that the control of the corporation can change hands easily and allows the controlling shareholder to benefit from the sale of control without damaging the minority shareholders.

- Some courts hold that a controlling shareholder violates his fiduciary duties when he fails to reveal the terms of his sale to the minority shareholders whom he deals with while selling his shares at a premium. Therefore, the controlling shareholder cannot pressure the minority shareholders into selling him their shares at an inferior price so that he can resell them to the purchaser at a premium.

i) **A.L.I. § 5.16** holds that a controlling shareholder has the right to sell the control at a premium unless:

   1. He does not disclose the transaction to the other shareholders whom he deals with in the sale; or
   2. The purchaser is likely to violate the duty of fair dealing.

ii) **What defines corporate control:**

   - A director has not breached any duty if he sells his shares at a premium, as long as he acts in good faith.
   - A director has the right of any other shareholder to deal freely with his stock.
   - The largest shareholder owes no special duty if he is not also the controlling majority shareholder.

iii) **Sale of Corporate office**

   Generally, the corporate directors can not sell their corporate office. However, as part of a sale of a controlling share of stocks, the sellers will often promise that the existing director(s) will resign, so that the new controlling shareholder can elect a new Board.

   - This is only allowed *if the shareholder sells a sufficient percentage of the corporations stock* to ensure that the purchaser's nominees can be elected.
   - If a shareholder controls the Board but does not own a controlling percentage of the shares, he can not sell his corporate office along with his non-controlling shares at a premium price. If he does, the control premium belongs to the corporation and the purchaser's Board "nominees" are void (*See Caplan v. Lionel Corp.*, 20 A.2d 301 (N.Y. 1969) (holding that a sale of office with only 3% of the shares is an invalid sale of office); *see also Brecher v. Gregg*, 392 N.Y.S.2d 776 (1975) (holding a shareholder who sold a corporate office with only 4% of the stock was required to hand over the premium to the corporation).

Essex Universal Corporation v. Yates, 305 F.2d
572 (2d Cir. 1962)

Facts: Yates, a shareholder who owned 28.3% of the
voting stock of a corporation. Yates contracted with Essex
to sell his shares. Part of the agreement was that Yates
would facilitate the resignation of the existing board
members and the election of Essex's choice of directors.
Yates tried to renege on the contract claiming that it was an
illegal sale of corporate office.

Held: This is not an illegal sale of corporate office. While
a bare sale of corporate office is not allowed, if it is
*combined with a controlling block of stock, it will be
allowed.* If control is purchased, there is no reason why the
new controlling shareholder cannot be vested with the
control at the beginning of the sale, therefore, it can be part
of the contract. Otherwise, it would be unreasonable to
prevent a group who purchases a controlling block of stock
from taking control right away.

Concurrence: (Friendly, CJ): Agrees that a sale of
control should allow a sale of corporate office, however
28% is not a sale of control because not all stockholders
would know that it is a transfer of control. Thus, it is an
insufficient percentage to circumvent a Board election.
Thus, corporate office should only be sold if there is a
majority (over 50%) of the shares sold.

iv)   **What is a sufficient percent of the shares?**
The controlling shareholder must own either a majority
(51%) or a large enough block of shares to ensure
"working control." This is generally an issue of fact
that will be determined on a case by case basis. In *Yates,*
28.3% was sufficient. In a later case, 9.7% was considered
a sufficient percentage. *See Carter v. Muscat*, 21 A.2d 543
(N.Y. 1964). However this case was unusual because, for

the most part, a sale of less than 20% will be insufficient. *See Treadway Companies, Inc. v. Care Corp.*, 683 F.2d 357 (2d Cir. 1980) (holding that 14% was an insufficient percentage to have a sale of control); *see also Caplan v. Lionel Corp.*, 20 A.2d 301 (NY 1969)(holding that 3% was an insufficient percentage for a sale of control).

b.   Who keeps the premium?

>   (i) No sharing rule:
>   - Generally, shareholders can sell at any price they wish.
>   - There is *no need to share* the premium.
>   - *Zetlin v. Hanson Holdings, Inc.*, 397 N.E.2d 387 (NY 1979) (holding that absent looting, conversion of corporate opportunity, fraud or any other bad faith action, a controlling shareholder is free to sell and a purchaser is free to buy controlling interest at a premium price).
>
>   (ii) Exceptions to the no share rule
>   - Can't sell the corporate office (*Bare Sale of Office*);
>   - Can't appropriate an offer to the corporation or the shareholders;
>   - Can't sell to looters; and
>   - Can't deprive the corporation of profits.

4. Sale to Looters

A controlling shareholder may not sell if he has reason to believe the buyer will loot the corporation. This is an intentional requirement--thus there is only a breach of the fiduciary duty if there a sufficient facts that would put a prudent person on notice that the purchaser is likely to loot the corporation.

i) **What facts are sufficient to show that the purchaser is likely to loot the corporation?**
A shareholder has no duty to investigate, however, the terms of the sale may give the seller inquiry notice. If the corporation has extremely liquid assets and very little goodwill, but, still the purchaser offers an unusually high premium, there are sufficient factors to put a reasonable person on notice that the purchaser intends to loot the company.

ii) **Warning signs triggering duty**
- The price is unusually high - $6 million for a $4 million value in shares - usually shows that the purchaser will loot the corporation to make up the difference.
- The purchaser can't afford the company - buys on credit and therefore will sell assets to pay back.
- The purchaser is dishonest or hurried - make further inquiries. If no interest is shown in the corporation investigate the purchasers motives.
- The purchaser has a bad reputation - significant debts, etc.

Solution:
Use due diligence: find out the buyers intentions, get a *certificate of intention,* put it into a contract that a breach of the intention is a ground for damages or for indemnification for liability to the shareholders.

iii) **Remedies for knowingly selling to a looter**
A controlling shareholder will usually be required to hand the control premium over to the minority shareholders and to reimburse the minority shareholders for any damages caused by the looting (i.e., loss of future profits, etc.).

Swinney v. Keebler Co., 480 F.2d 573 (4th Cir. 1973)
Facts: Atlantic offered to purchase the shares of the Meadows corporation from Keebler, a majority shareholder. There were no indications that Atlantic would loot the corporation, it was a solid corporation, had sufficient funds to make the purchase and run Meadows, and agreed to guarantee Meadows' outstanding debt. However shortly after the sale, Atlantic sold Meadows and Meadows eventually went bankrupt. The debt holder's sued Keebler claiming that it breached its fiduciary duty by failing to see that Atlantic intended to loot Meadows.

Held: There was no breach of fiduciary duty.
The majority has a duty to ensure that others are not injured by foreseeable harms from their actions. However, there is no fiduciary duty in a mere sale unless fraud or intent to loot is foreseen.
There is no duty to investigate absent suspicion.
If there is suspicion of looting there is either an obligation not to sell or an obligation to investigate the foreseen looting to ensure under the reasonable man standard that there is none.

Gerdes v. Reynolds, 28 N.Y.S.2d 622 (1941)
Facts: Majority shareholders (who were also directors) sold their shares for a premium. The purchasers did not fully pay for the shares. The majority shareholders neither investigated the purchasers nor informed the minority shareholders. The majority shareholders also resigned as directors and appointed the purchaser's nominees to the board.

Held: The shareholders breached their fiduciary duty when they left the corporation in the hands of the purchasers, knowing that they did not have sufficient funds to pay for the shares. This was a sure sign of looting that required a reasonable person to investigate.

DeBaun v. First Western Bank & Trust Co., 46 Cal. App. 3d 686 (1975)
Facts: First Western, a controlling shareholder sold their interest in the corporation. The purchaser had a past history of financial troubles including bankruptcy. However, First Western did not investigate the purchaser's resources and motives. Shortly after the sale, the purchaser looted the corporation which ended up insolvent.

Held: First Western breached its fiduciary duty. It was on sufficient notice that the purchaser intended to loot the corporation and failed to investigate or refrain from selling.

5. **Appropriate of an offer to the corporation or the shareholders**

If a purchaser offers to buy all of the corporation's assets or to merge with the corporation, a controlling shareholder can not convince the purchaser to buy all of his shares instead at a premium. This is especially true in the case where the controlling shareholder sells his shares and then aids the purchaser in buying the minority shares at an inferior price.
- If this is done, the shareholder must pay the premium over to the corporation or the minority shareholders.
- *See e.g., Brown v. Halbert*, 271 Cal. App. 2d 252 (1969) (holding that a controlling shareholder will breach his fiduciary duties when he diverts an offer to buy the entire corporation into an offer to

purchase his shares at a large premium and then
pressures the minority shareholders into accepting
an inferior price).

* *See also Roby v. Dunnett*, 88 F.2d 68 (10th Cir.),
cert. den'd, 301 U.S. 706 (1937).

a. **Can't Deprive the Corporation of a Profit**
A controlling shareholder cannot a divert corporate
opportunity or profits from the minority shareholders unless
the profit is earned through the shareholder's own efforts.
The controlling shareholder cannot use his control to
prevent the corporation from receiving profits it would have
otherwise obtained.

Perlman v. Feldman, 219 F.2d 173 (2d Cir.), *cert
den'd*, 349 U.S. 952 (1955)
Facts: A controlling shareholder (37%--who was also a
director) sold his shares in a steel corporation for a
premium. There was no deliberate fraud or looting by the
purchaser's; however the sale included the right to purchase
the corporation's steel at extremely low prices. This greatly
decreased the corporation's profits and cash flow.

Held: This was a breach of fiduciary duty because the
controlling shareholder knew that the sale would lead to a
loss of profitability to the corporation and the minority
shareholders.

B.   The Merger Process: Steps to a Hostile Takeover

1.   The Target

    a.   Choose a target

    b.   Choosing a Takeover Method (See infra Rule 10b-5 PSLRA for more later)

        1)   **Proxy battle** (discussed *supra*).

        2)   **Tender offer** - an offer by a bidder sent to the shareholders of the target corporation to purchase their shares for cash or securities. It is usually targeted to all or at least a majority of the shareholders.

            a)   *Two tiered* **offer:** The bidder purchases less than 100% of the shares at one price (the first tier) and then announces the first tier's success before purchasing the second tier. If the first tier has a higher price, it is a front loaded tender offer. This will coerce shareholders to buy now or risk a lower price in the future. If the second tier has a higher price, it is a back loaded tender offer.

            b)   **Any and all cash offers (LBO):** This is where a bidder forms a corporation, receives a bridge loan from financiers, obtains control of the target, merges with the corporation and then pays back the loan with the target's assets.

c. **Silently Purchase a Percentage, then Announce Hostile Takeover**

This prevents shareholder's from quickly selling since they will hold out for more money.

d. **Target Defenses** (See infra Rule 16b: Short Swing Profits for examples of defenses)

1) **Revise the corporate governance structure**
   - *Shark repellents* - make changing control drawn out and expensive.
   - *Stagger the Board* - delays change in composition.
   - Only allow the Board to call Special Shareholder meeting.
   - Eliminate shareholder power to act without a meeting.
   - Amend the charter for a supermajority approval of mergers and combinations (this is especially good if corporation owns a lot of stock).
   - Amend charter to require a back end fair price.
   - Anti-green mail amendment **Green mail** -- a payment by a potential target to a potential bidder to buy back shares that have been purchased--usually at a premium. The bidder in exchange will agree not to pursue a takeover bid.

2) **Revise corporations capital structure**
   Most can be done without shareholder approval and either give equity to shareholder or create new debt making the corporation less attractive to bidders. This may cause duty of loyalty problems.

Self tender - Target offers to repurchase its stock for cash or securities. Borrow the money needed to increase the corporation's leverage.

Market sweep - Target can buy its own shares on the open market.

Poison pill - give shareholders the right to purchase stock at huge discounts upon a triggered event. The pill will always be redeemable by management before triggering event.

- **Flip-Over Poison Pill**-- The shareholder's right is triggered when an outsider buys a certain percentage of the target's stock.
- **Flip-in Poison Pill**- Gives the existing shareholders the right to buy shares of the target at a cheap price.
- **Back-end Poison Pill** --fixes a fair price for the shares and requires that the company buy shareholders' shares at that price if the bidder doesn't do so, after it obtains control. This removes coercion from the second tier of a tender offer.
- **Lollipop rights** --Allows the shareholders to redeem shares not purchased in tender offer at a set price.

3) **Alter the shareholder mix**

Increase the proportion of shareholders sympathetic to or controlled by management.

There must be *compelling business reasons* to do this.

- **White Squire**- The target solicits tender offers from other bidders who are more "friendly" to management.
- **ESOP-** The Employee Stock Ownership Plan can purchase shares.

- Since these plans are owned (or at least
  controlled) by management this is a great of
  interest.
- **Lock up**-Protects a "friendly" bidder from a
  hostile bidder by giving an option to acquire assets
  at a bargain price under certain circumstances.

4) **Find a "friendly" bidder**
   One who is likely to maintain management.
   - Ask a **White Knight** to bid.
   - **Management Leverage Buy-Out** - bid for
     its own company through debt.
   - **No Shop clause**--an agreement between the
     target and a friendly bidder that prevents the
     target from giving information or soliciting
     other bidders to assure that the White Knight
     will succeed.

5) **Buy new Business or sell existing
   businesses**
   Many do not need shareholder approval and they make
   the target less attractive.

6) **Scorched Earth defenses**
   (i) **Asset lockup** - gives a White Knight the
       option to buy assets or a portion of the
       business at bargain prices.
   (ii) **Crown Jewel**--Gives a White Knight a lock-
        up provision that allows the Knight to
        purchase the target's most desirable part of its
        business. This removes reasons for a takeover
        because the target is no longer as coveted.
   (iii) Target buys a new business or property that
         will create an anti trust or regulatory problem
         for the bidder.

7) **Accelerate or increase management's employment benefits**

Golden parachute- assure severance pay for senior management if there is a takeover. This will increase the cost of takeovers or soften the blows if they succeed.

8) **Buy out the bidder**
   - Target can pay **green mail** to buy the bidder's shares at a premium. Often called a **Share repurchase**.

   - **Standstill agreement** -- obligates the green mailer not to acquire any more shares for a specific time period.
     Temporarily ends the threat.

9) **Attack the Bidder**
   - **Pacman defense** - begin a tender offer for the bidder's company.
   - Sue the bidder for violating antitrust merger guidelines or state anti-takeover rules.

e. **Takeover Benefits**
    - Shareholders gain a lot of money.
    - New management team will do better for the company.
    - *Synergy*- combined firms have higher value.
    - *Market Myopia*- stock markets undervalue companies thus this allows shareholders to benefit from the companies true value.

f. **Corporate detriments**
- **Empire Building**- The bidder wants large companies so that compensation for management is greater. Shareholders of the bidder are harmed.
- **Goring** - Shareholders gain at the employees, creditors, customers and taxpayers expense.

2. **How to acquire the target**
Valuation of the target, will determine the price.

a. The means of valuation
1) **Book value**: Assets minus liabilities of corporation. However, this means cannot value intangible items such as goodwill.

2) **Capitalized Earning**: earning potential is reflected.

3) **Appraisal rights:** Appraisal rights are remedies for shareholders who dissent to extraordinary transactions such as mergers, sales of all or substantially all of the assets, and consolidations. They require the corporation to buy the dissenter's shares at the price immediately before the transaction occurs.
- The purpose of appraisal rights is to allow shareholders who dissent to a transaction to receive the fair value of their shares.
- Shareholders must give notice of their intent to dissent.
- Shareholders waive dissenters rights if they vote for or consent to the merger.
- Acquiring shareholders do not always get appraisal rights because their rights are not always affected.

- Acquired corporations always get appraisal rights since their rights are always affected.
  Many merger type transactions known as *de facto* mergers seek to avoid appraisal rights--*see infra.*

4) **Initial Agreement:** By agreement the value is set. This is very impartial because the agreement does not reflect the actual valuation.
   - Some require re-evaluation every year.
   - Retirement provisions.

b.   Exceptions

RMBCA	DGCL
§13.02(a)(1) No Market Price Exclusion •Market price may not reflect true value: • Market price only shows earning power. • Not full value if corporation's liquidation value exceeds it.	**§262(b)(1) - Appraisal Rights** •No rights if the corporation is publicly traded.

Look to the chart at end of this section to see when shareholders have appraisal and voting rights.

c.   **Mergers**

There are 5 types of mergers
1) Statutory
2) Consolidation
3) Short-form
4) Triangular
5) Squeeze out

P = Purchaser; T = Target; S= subsidiary corporation

1) **Statutory Merger** (RMBCA § 11; DGCL §251(a))
   - Statutory mergers occur when one corporation (**P**) acquires another (**T**) and the acquired corporation (**T**) no longer exists *complete absorption.*
   - The surviving corporation "steps into the shoes" of the acquired corporation and **P** now owns all of **T's** assets and assumes all of **T's** liabilities and contracts.
   - **T's** shareholder's are paid in cash, stock of **P**, property or a combination by the **P** corporation.
   - A *consolidation* is similar to a statutory merger except **P** & **T** merge into a new corporation instead of **P**.

   (i)   **Steps to a statutory merger:**
      (a) The Boards of **P** & **T** adopt plan of merger. (RMBCA §11.01, DGCL § 251(b)); which contains the following provisions:
      The Boards must:
         1)   Designate which corporation (here **P**) is to survive the merger;
         2)   Describe the terms and conditions of the merger;
         3)   Describe the manner in which shares of **T** will be converted into shares of **P** (on other property, such as cash or bonds);

182

4) Set forth any amendments to P's articles of incorporation necessary to effectuate the plan of merger or that the articles will remain the same; and

5) Set forth any other necessary provisions.

(b) Submit plan of merger to the shareholders of *both* **P & T**. (RMBCA § 11.03, DGCL § 251(c))
   1) Approval by a majority of shareholders-- unless the articles require a higher vote.
   2) Shareholders must be notified with the purpose of the special meeting.

Small Scale Statutory Merger - one that increases **P**'s outstanding voting stock by more than 20% - **P**'s shareholders are not required to vote and shareholders have no dissenters rights. (RMBCA 11.03(g), DGCL 251(f)).

(i) After any required shareholder approval is secured, the plan of merger is filed with an appropriate state office and the merger becomes effective. No formal conveyance or assignment need to be executed.

(ii) By operation of law, **T** immediately ceases to exist.

(iii) Former shareholders of **T** automatically become shareholders of **P**; they also lose all rights they had as shareholders of **T**, unless they dissent and seek appraisal of their shares. (RMBCA § 11.06, DGCL § 259).

(iv) Shareholders of **P** retain their rights as shareholders of the surviving corporation, but they, also, are entitled to dissenter's rights. (RMBCA § 13.02, DGCL § 262).

2)   Consolidation
- Very close to a statutory merger.
- Two companies combine into a new corporation.
- The same rules that apply for statutory mergers apply for consolidations..

3)   Short-form Merger
A merger of a subsidiary into a parent through a procedure permitted by the RMBCA and the statutes of many states. **P** owns at least 90% of **T's** stock prior to the merger- No vote by the shareholders of **P** or **T** is required. Only **T's** shareholders have appraisal rights.
(RMBCA § 11.04, DGCL § 253).

4)   Triangular Merger: P loses voting rights
(i)   Used to avoid legal consequences associated with statutory mergers. (In a statutory merger, P acquires all of T's liabilities).
(ii)   Often used when P does not want to absorb T--it wants to keep **T** as a subsidiary.
    (1)   **P** creates a subsidiary corporation **S**.
    (2)   **P** gives **S** the merger shares or merger consideration in exchange for all of **S's** shares.

A triangle merger can be done in two ways:
    (1)   **Reverse merger** - **S** into **T, T** survives. This is usually done if **T** has rights under contracts, leases, etc. that it will lose if it does not survive the merger.
    (2)   **Forward merger** - **T** into **S, S** survives.
- S & T follow the steps necessary to effectuate a statutory merger: the Boards of **S** & **T** adopt the plan of merger; the shareholders of **S** & **T** both vote to

approve the merger; and **T** is then merged into S by operation of law.

* Shareholders of both **S** & **T** both have *voting and appraisal rights.*
* **S** is fully owned by **P**, so **P**'s Board can vote as the shareholders.
* **P**'s shareholders cannot vote since they are not a party to the merger.

5)   Squeeze Out Merger

    (i)   Allows a controlling shareholder to rid the corporation of minority shareholders.

    (ii) This is usually, the second step in a takeover, the first being obtaining a controlling interest in stock.

    (iii) The corporation is merged into a parent corporation where the controlling stockholder holds power. Then, the plan of merger is set up in favor of the parent stockholder. The parent receives the subsidiary stock and the remaining shareholders receive other consideration such as nonvoting debt securities. If the minority subsidiary stockholders receive cash instead, it is called a ***buy-out or cash-out merger.***

d.   Exchange of Stock for Assets

P uses its stock (or some combination of stock, cash and other securities) to buy the assets of **T**.

P may, but need not, also assume some or all of T's liabilities. Alternatively, **T** may retain sufficient liquid assets to pay off its liabilities.

    (i)   Approval of an agreement of sale by the Boards of both **P** & **T** is required. (RMBCA § 12.02, DGCL § 271).

    (ii) The shareholders of **T**, the selling corporation, but not the shareholders of **P**, the acquiring corporation must approve the terms of the asset sale agreement.

    (iii) **T** dissolves and liquidates--**T** disappears and T's shareholders are now **P** shareholders.

    (iv) Under RMBCA § 13.02(a)(3), T's shareholders will have dissenter's rights if they vote against the transaction. If **T** is a Delaware corporation, though, dissenter's rights will not be available. (DGCL § 262).

1)   Successor Liability Doctrine

In an exchange of shares or a stock for assets merger, some courts impose liability on **P** for unknown or contingent claims at the time the assets were sold. *See Turner v. Bituminous Casualty Co.,* 244 N.W.2d 873 (Mich. 1976) (holding the purchaser liable if it continued to manufacture the seller's product line); *but see Niccum v. Hydra Tool Corp.,* 428 N.W.2d 96 (Minn. 1989) (holding that there is no liability unless there is continuity in management, business assets, and the selling shareholders)).

e.   **Exchange of Shares for Stock**
(only available under RMBCA § 11.02)

P buys all of **T**'s shares in exchange for shares of **P.**

   (i)   The Boards of **P** & **T** must approve an agreement.
          (RMBCA § 11.02).
   (ii) Only shareholders of **T** (not **P**), must approve the plan of
          exchange. (RMBCA § 11.03).
   (iii) Once approved, the plan of exchange is filed and shares of **P**
          are issued to the shareholders of **T** (unless the plan calls for
          use of cash, or other property).
   (iv) **T**'s former shareholders thereby become shareholders of **P**;
          they have no further rights as shareholders of **T**, unless they
          dissent and seek appraisal of their stock. (RMBCA §
          11.06).
   (v)   Upon effectuation of a exchange, **T** becomes a subsidiary of
          P.
          If **P** doesn't want to operate **T** as a subsidiary, but wishes to
          end with precisely the same structure as would result from
          merging **T** into **P**, it can follow the exchange of shares by:

   •   Dissolving **T**, distributing all of its assets to **P** and,
       Having **P** assume all of its liabilities; or

   •   Merging **T** into **P** in a "*short form*" merger.

f.   *Defacto* **Merger**
       Many courts hold that stock for stock and stock for asset
       combinations are in effect mergers and are merely used to avoid
       the shareholder's voting and appraisal rights.

       The defacto merger doctrine states that if **P** acquires all
       of **T**'s assets and assumes **T**'s liabilities for **P**'s stock or
       acquires all of **T**'s stock for **P**'s stock, **P**'s shareholders must
       approve the transaction and dissenters will have appraisal
       rights. (*See Applestein v. United Board & Carton Co.*, 159

A.2d 146 (N.J. 1960); *Ferris v. Glen Alden Corp.*, 143 A.2d 25 (Pa 1958)).

Delaware courts have rejected this rule and does not provide merger protection for shareholders since the statute doesn't provide it. (*See Hariton v. Arco Electronics, Inc.*, 182 A.2d 22 (Del. Ch. 1962), *aff'd*, 188 A.2d 123 (Del 1963)).

g.   Tender Offer
(only available under DE law)

(i)   Replaces a share exchange.

(ii)   **P** can seek to acquire **T** by offering to purchase **T**'s shares directly from the **T** shareholders, either for **P** stock or for cash or other property or some combination.

(iii) **P** can acquire control of **T** without a vote of the **T** Board. Although the tender offer may be part of a friendly transaction approved by both Boards .

(iv)   **T** shareholders "approve" the transaction by accepting P's offer rather than through a formal vote.

- There are no dissenters' rights; **T** shareholders who wish to disapprove do so by refusing to tender their shares.
- **P** can make a tender offer without any vote by its shareholders, unless **P** does not have sufficient stock authorized to effectuate a proposed share exchange.
- **P**'s shareholders also will not have dissenters' rights in the tender offer.

Example: *QVC v. Paramount*

Two steps:

1. Obtain a majority of T's shares, at least 51% through a public tender offer.
2. Purchase the remainder of the stock:
   - Short Form or Statutory Merger;
     No dissenters' rights will be available in Delaware since the shareholders can sell on the public market.

3. Summary of Voting and Appraisal Rights

Merger type	P-surviving Vote	Dissenters Rights	T-acquired Vote	Dissenters Rights
Statutory	RMBCA - **Yes** 11.03 ---------------- DGCL - **Yes** 251	RMBCA - **Yes** 13.02 ---------------- DGCL - Yes 262 (unless 262(b)(1) applies)	RMBCA - **Yes** 11.03 ---------------- DGCL - **Yes** 251	RMBCA - **Yes** 13.02 ---------------- DGCL - Yes 262 (unless 262(b)(1) applies)
Triangular	RMBCA - **NO** ---------------- DGCL - **NO**	RMBCA - **NO** ---------------- DGCL - **NO**	RMBCA - **Yes** 11.03 ---------------- DGCL - **Yes** 251	RMBCA - **Yes** 13.02 ---------------- DGCL - Yes 262 (unless 262(b)(1) applies
Statutory Share Exchange	RMBCA - **NO** 11.03 ---------------- DGCL -**N.A.**	RMBCA - **NO** 13.02 ---------------- DGCL - **N.A**	RMBCA - **Yes** 11.03 ---------------- DGCL - **N.A**	RMBCA - **Yes** 13.02 ---------------- DGCL -**N.A.**
Stock for Assets	RMBCA - **N o** ---------------- DGCL - **NO**	RMBCA - **NO** ---------------- DGCL - **NO**	RMBCA - **Yes** 12.02 ---------------- DGCL - **Yes** 271	RMBCA - **Yes** 13.02 ---------------- DGCL - **NO**

Note: *Stock market **exception***
If the shares of a corporation are sold on a public capital market, there are no appraisal rights because the shareholders can sell them on the free market.

189

C. Contests for Control

This section deals with a situation where an entity (shareholders, directors, third party) wishes to take control of the corporation. Very often there is a hostile situation as a "contest" between the parties wishing to take over control.

- A **hostile takeover** is one in which the target's Board is opposed to the merger.
- A **friendly takeover** is one in which the takeover is supported by the target's Board.

1. **Defense Theories**- - whether the board can take defensive measures to a hostile bid.
   a. **Passive** (Assumes an interested Board)[
      - There is always a *conflict of interest* when there is a hostile takeover. The Board still has fiduciary duties to the shareholders, but they also wish *to prevent themselves from being ousted by the new owners.*
      - Thus, while the shareholders wish to receive premium bids, the directors and management may wish to oppose hostile bids.

      Note: The passive arguments state that *management* should *not use corporate funds to impose obstacles to takeovers.* Any such obstacles will dissuade bidders, thereby crimping the market for the shareholders.

   b. **Active** (Assumes a disinterested Board)
      - The Board must be able to negotiate to prevent coercive bidding on the voiceless shareholders.
      - Board action will prevent destructive bids, buy time and increase shareholders' profit.

2. Defense measures to a takeover: Revlon

Revlon v. MacAndrews & Forbes Holdings, Inc., 506
A.2d 173 (Del. 1986)

Facts: Pantry Pride corporation attempted a hostile takeover of Revlon. Revlon's Board took action to thwart the tender offer. The defenses included bidding with Forstmann, a white knight, and eventually giving Forstmann a lock-up on key assets and a no-shop provision (it appeared that the Board was making these defenses to protect Revlon's note holders). However, despite all of these efforts, the tender offer became inevitable. MacAndrews, the controlling stockholder of Pantry Pride was granted an injunction to prevent Revlon's board from continuing the defensive measures. Revlon appealed the injunction.

Held: The injunction was upheld. Directors are allowed to take defensive measures when they feel a takeover bid is not in the corporation's best interest without violating their fiduciary duties. Thus, the defensive measures taken were in and of themselves legal However, as soon as the dissolution or sale of the corporation becomes inevitable, their duties shift and they must try to get the shareholders the best possible price. They can no longer try to protect the corporation or other constituencies. Thus, Revlon defines the UNOCAL standard--it changes when the sale becomes inevitable.

Rule: As soon as a sale or dissolution of the corporation is inevitable, things change

No more defensive mechanisms - The Board becomes an auctioneer and attempts to get the highest shareholder price.

Tilted Playing Field - The Board owes no duty to the potential suitors and, therefore, does not need to deal with them on equal footing as long as it is

achieving the best results for the shareholder.
However, the Board can no longer favor other
constituents over shareholders.

In Revlon, that sale was inevitable because it became
apparent that the corporation was going to be sold either to
the bidder or the white knight.

Other cases have held that *a sale is inevitable when*:
   a)   A corporation initiates an active bidding process or
        seeks to break itself up.
   b)   There is a sale or change of control other than
        ordinary sales in the public market.
   c)   The corporation changes its long term goals and
        separates its assets.
   d)   If the Board places the corporation up for auction or
        begins a sale process that says we are for sale.
   e)   *See, e.g., Arnold v. Society for Savings Bancorp,
        Inc.*, 650 A.2d 1270 (Del. 1994); *see also Mills
        Acquisition Co., v. Macmillian, Inc.*, 559 A.2d 34
        (Del. Super. Ct. 1989).

3. Bidding, the fair auction and the BJR : MacMillon

Mills v. MacMillon, Inc., 559 A.2d 34 (Del. Super. Ct.
1989).
   Facts: MacMillan, Inc. was the target of a bidding war
   between two entities: KKR and Mills. It was inevitable that
   the corporation would be sold, therefore under Revlon, the
   directors of MacMillan were under enhanced duties to obtain
   the highest bid possible. Two of MacMillan's directors
   (who had a combined 20% interest in KKR winning) leaked
   information to KKR and mislead Mills about the bidding.
   Thus, Mills thought it entered the highest bid and did not
   increase the amount of their offer. KKR won the auction
   and Mills sought to invalidate the auction.

192

Held: The directors violated their duty of care. By failing to conduct a fair auction, they could not rely on the Business Judgment Rule. Management cannot allow its choice of bidder to win unfairly, they must obtain the highest bid for the shareholders. Here, they improperly tipped the scales by purposely misleading the hostile party (Mills), imposing short deadlines, and refusing to negotiate with both parties.

Rule:

1. A Board will breach its fiduciary duty if it allows the interested bidders' management to control the auction. Thus the Board should *utilize independent director committees.*

2. A board may tip the playing field towards one bidder as long as the overall goal is to obtain more money for the shareholder.

3. The Board's main goal must be to get the *"Highest value reasonably obtainable for shareholder provided that it was offered by a responsible and reputable bidder."* To do this look at:
   - Fairness and feasibility of the bid.
   - Proposed finances and consequences of the transaction.
   - Impact on the shareholders and related constituents.
   - Risk of non consummation.
   - Shareholder interests at stake.
   - Bidder's identity and background.
   - Bidder's plans for the corporation.

4. Shareholders best interest in a merger and the BJR: Paramount v. Time

Paramount Communications, Inc. v. Time Incorporated, 571 A.2d 1140 (Del. Super. Ct. 1990)

Facts: Time and Warner negotiated a merger after both companies determined that it would be the best long term strategy for each company. After sending proxy materials to their shareholders, although not required under DGCL), Time wished to have shareholder approval. Paramount began a tender offer for all of Time's shares. The tender offer was conditioned upon Time discontinuing the Warner merger. Time's Board (relying on financial and business advisors) decided that the Warner deal was better for the shareholders and that the paramount bid was inadequate (even after the price was increased). Time was afraid shareholders would not see how good a deal Warner is and, therefore, initiated a reverse triangle merger -- a "friendly" all cash tender offer for 51% of Warner combined with a back end merger made up of cash and securities. This prevented Time shareholders from being able to vote on the merger, and prevented the paramount takeover, but imposed a significant debt on Time. Paramount challenged the merger contending that the Time-Warner deal was a sale, therefore Revlon duties should apply.

Held: The Time board did not breach their fiduciary duties.

1. The board approved the merger before the Paramount tender offer began, therefore the decision was within the Business Judgment Rule's protection. Here the directors determined that the merger would diversify Time and therefore be the best long run strategy for the corporation.

2. Additionally, although the defensive strategy to change the plan of merger did fall under UNOCAL's enhanced

194

scrutiny. Time satisfied this test also because the Board's decision was informed and the Board was acting in the shareholder's best interest. Unlike *UNOCAL*, here the second end of the merger was not coercive, therefore there is much less a threat to the shareholders.

3. The court accepted the Board's argument that the Paramount deal was inadequate therefore, it was all right to take the vote away from the shareholders'. Additionally, the combination was not final Paramount could purchase the combined corporation. There is no requirement that the Board terminate a long-term well-thought-out plan for a short term shareholder benefit.

4. *This was not a sale under Revlon.* There was no change in control since there was a *fluid aggregation of public owners* before and after the deal, therefore **no** Revlon duties.

   Revlon duties will only be triggered if:
   a. There is an attempt to break up company - unilaterally or through hostile takeover defenses.
   b. The corporation begins an active bidding process because a sale is inevitable.

5. Duty to get the best value: Paramount v. QVC

Paramount Communications, Inc. v. QVC Network, Inc., 637 A.2d 34 (Del. 1994)

Facts: Paramount & Viacom agreed to a merger for cash and stock. The merger would constitute a change in control of Paramount because Viacom would be purchasing about 20% of its stock. Paramount amended its poison pill and granted a no-shop, stock lockup and termination fee to Viacom. This made it almost impossible for another party to bid successfully on Paramount or break up the merger. QVC initiated a two step tender offer for Paramount for both cash and stock. This initiated a bidding auction. The

QVC offer was more lucrative for Paramount's shareholders, however Paramount's Board favored Viacom. As a result, there was not a level playing field because Paramount refused to remove or change the preference actions (no-shop, poison pill, termination fee) that it had granted to Viacom. QVC claimed that the Board's actions violated their fiduciary duties to the shareholders.

Held: The Board failed to exert the required enhanced scrutiny. This was a sale of control situation that required enhanced scrutiny of the Board's actions. Thus, the directors primary objective was to obtain the best value reasonably available for the shareholders. By failing to remove or change the defensive measures adopted--the lock up, the no shop and termination fee--the Paramount Board failed to fully inform themselves of the QVC deal and violated their duty to get the best value.

Rule:
1. In a sale the shareholders sell their voting control to a single buyer giving up their voting leverage. There is only one chance to do this, therefore the Board has a duty to evaluate and seek the best value reasonably available.
2. This type of transaction is subject to enhanced judicial scrutiny both in the process and the reasonableness of the Board's action.
3. Thus, the Revlon Duty to achieve the "best value" occurs when there will be a change in control.
4. Revlon does not necessarily require that there be an auction, however, the Board must be adequately informed and attempt to secure the best value available for the shareholder.
   - The judgment is subject to enhanced scrutiny.
   - Here, the Board failed miserably;

- The Board was unwilling to change its stance and negotiate with QVC;
- The Board believed that QVC was illusory without being informed;
- The Board closed its mind to other offers that could benefit shareholder.

6. Summary of the Delaware Fiduciary Duties in a Change of Control Situation--*Enhanced Scrutiny*

A director may rely on the Business Judgment Rule protection as long as:

a) The director used reasonable care in assessing the threat of a takeover before taking any actions to defend the corporation or thwart the takeover;

b) The Board adequately informs itself of all opportunities;

c) The responses that the Board makes to any takeover threats are reasonable in light of all circumstances;

d) If it is inevitable that there will be a sale or a change in control of the corporation, the Board ensures that the shareholders get the best valuable reasonably attainable (thus does not put its preferences above the shareholders needs);

e) Under the Duty of Loyalty, the directors must protect the shareholders over all other constituents including creditors, employees and the community when it is threatened with a takeover.

D.   Selling All or Substantially All of the Assets

1.   When is shareholders approval necessary?
Check *the charter and by-laws* for any special requirements.

RMBCA	DGCL
§12.01 - Sale of Assets in Regular Course of Business and Mortgage of Assets	**§271 - Sale, Lease or Exchange of Assets; Consideration; Procedure**
•No shareholder approval is needed to sell all or substantially all of the corporation's assets if it is in the regular course of business.	•Shareholder approval is required for the sale, lease or exchange of all or substantially all of the corporation's property and assets.
•The corporation can sell, lease, exchange, mortgage, pledge, dedicate, and transfer assets to a wholly-owned subsidiary without shareholder approval unless the articles of incorporation require approval.	•If not all or substantially all, then no approval needed. •Shareholder approval is the affirmative vote of a majority of the outstanding shares. •The corporation must give at least 20 days notice that a meeting to consider a proposal will occur.
	•The Board can abandon a plan to sell, lease or exchange the assets without shareholder approval.

198

RMBCA	DGCL

§12.02 - Sale of Assets Other Than in Regular Course of Business
•Shareholder approval is required if all or substantially all of the corporation's assets are to be sold outside of the ordinary course of business.
•To authorize a transaction:
  • The Board must recommend a proposal; and
  • The shareholders must approve the proposal.
•The Board can condition its proposal on any condition.
•The Board must give the shareholders notice of the meeting under **§ 7.05** with the stated purpose.
•The proposal must be approved by a majority of the outstanding shares unless the articles require a greater number.
•The board can abandon the transaction without the shareholder approval.
•The purchasing corporation does not necessarily need shareholder approval.	

a. RMBCA Definition of All or Substantially

- Substantially all = nearly all.
- Selling several distinct manufacturing lines while retaining others is **NOT** selling all or substantially all even if the lines include a significant fraction of the corporations business.
- If the lines retained are only temporary or are a pretext to avoid the test, then it is substantially all.
- Selling a manufacturing plant but retaining the operating assets (machinery, equipment, etc., accounts receivable and goodwill) is not selling substantially all of the assets.
- Look to the heart of the business.
- Selling the majority of the corporation's assets is substantially all.
- The RMBCA allows more discretion than the DGCL.

b. Delaware Common Law

Gimbel v. Signal Companies, Inc., 316 A.2d 599 (Del. Ch. 1974), *aff'd per curiam* 316 A.2d 619 (Del. 1974) **Facts:** A parent corporation sold a subsidiary which accounted for 41% of its net worth, 26% of its assets and 15% of its earnings.

Held: this was not a sale of substantially all of the corporation's assets. Absent a statutory requirement, the board may take all actions needed without shareholder approval and here there was no statutory requirement. The court laid out two tests to see if a sale is substantially all of the corporation's assets:

1. *Quantitative test* - the assets are substantial if they are quantitatively vital to the selling corporation's existence.
2. *Qualitative test* - sales causes a qualitative change in the business structure.

Note:
Shareholder approval is required if the sale is a radical
change in purpose or business.
Shareholder approval is required if the sale is not a typical
transaction in the regular course of business.
Gimbel was not "substantially all" of the assets since it was
only selling a division off that was 41% of the
corporation's net worth. Signal was a conglomerate that
sold assets and subsidiaries all the time therefore, the sale
was not a fundamental change in the business structure.

Katz v. Bregman, 431 A.2d 1274 (Del. Ch. 1981)
Facts: Corporation sold 51% of its assets and 45% of its
net sales to start a new business line.

Held: The approval was needed.

Rule: Look to see if the sold assets constitute substantially
all of the corporation's revenues and operating assets and
whether the assets sold are vital to corporations business.

2. **Appraisal Rights** are pertinent in all change of control
   situations; a means to allow the shareholders who disagree with
   the sale of all or substantially all of the corporation's assets to be
   paid a fair value of the stock.

RMBCA	**DGCL**
§13.02 **(a)(3)** ● Allows appraisal rights for sale of all or substantially all of the corporation's assets.	**§262** ● No appraisal rights are available for the sale of all or substantially all of the corporation's assets.

a. **Procedure:**
- **Notice by the Corporation** - The corporation must notify all shareholders of record, not less than 20 days prior to a meeting called to vote on a merger, that appraisal rights are available.
- **Notice by Shareholders** - A shareholder must notify the corporation in writing before the vote is taken that he wishes to exercise his appraisal rights, and he must NOT vote for the merger. Within 10 days after the merger becomes effective, the surviving corporation shall notify all shareholders demanding appraisal.

- **Demand for Payment** - Once the acquisition or merger is approved, the shareholder must demand payment and deposit his shares with the corporation.

- Shareholders must follow the statutory procedures precisely in order to obtain the appraisal value.

- The Court will determine which shareholders have complied with the statutory requirements and the value of the shares.

VII. SECURITIES REGULATION: An Introduction

A. Underwriting Securities and Federal and State Regulations

1. Underwriting

Underwriting is the process by which a securities dealer takes stock from a corporate issuer and arranges for its sale to the public.

> **Statutory Regulation**: Underwriters are subject to strict regulation under both federal and state laws:
> 1. Generally require full disclosure of compensation agreements;
> 2. Subject the underwriter to the same anti-fraud prohibitions applicable to the issuer.

a. Firm Commitment Underwriting: Underwriters purchase the entire issue from the corporation and market the shares to the public.

b. Best Efforts Underwriting: Underwriters are bound only to use their best efforts to sell the stock and are not responsible to the corporation for unsold stock.

2. Statutes Regulating Issuance of Shares

State and federal laws regulate the issuance of securities. Since federal laws do not preempt the filing (Securities Act of 1933 §18), a corporate issuer must often comply with both state and federal regulations.

a. **State Regulation - Blue Sky Laws:** State statutes regulating the issuance of securities preventing "schemes which have no more basis than so many feet of blue sky". *Hall v. Geiger-Jones Co.*, 242 U.S. 539, 37, S.Ct 217

    (1) **Three basic types of blue sky laws** (states combine the features of more than one type in connection with issuance of securities):
        (i) **Fraud Type** - Civil or criminal penalties.
        (ii) **License Type** - Requires registration and submission of information by all sellers, securities-brokers, dealers, and agents of corporate issuers.
        (iii) **Securities Registration Type** - requires that prior to issuance all stocks be registered (or qualified) with the appropriate state office or agency. Securities Registration is the most comprehensive type of blue sky law.

    (2) **Registration**
        (i) **Registration by Notification** - (disclosure) Requires complete description of both the issuer and the shares to be issued, and the shares must be sold as described. Generally states do not deny permission to issue stock.
        (ii) **Registration by Qualification** - After substantive review, a state official can prevent issuance if it fails to meet statutory requirements.
        (iii) **Registration by Coordination** - State provides that securities registered under the federal requirements may be issued by submitting the same information to the state.

b. Issuance of Securities Under Federal Regulation: The Securities Act of 1933 (15 U.S.C. §77)

- Structures the distribution of securities through the mails or by the use of interstate commerce.
- Establishes by regulation a comprehensive **registration type system**, which provides the *full disclosure of all pertinent facts.*
- The Securities and Exchange Commission (SEC) does not have the power to disapprove a proposed issuance.
- The SEC is charged only to enforce the federal disclosure regulations.

1. **Registration Statement**: **Securities Act §5(c).**
    Forbids the use of interstate facilities or the mails to offer to sell a security, unless a registration statement has been filed with and declared effective by the SEC.

    (i)   **Waiting Period**: **Securities Act §5(b)(1).**
          During the time (waiting period) between the filing of the registration statement and the effective date, no written offer to sell a security may be made through the mails or interstate commerce.

    (ii) **Effective Date** The date the proposed issuance and Registration Statement meets the registration requirements for a statutory prospectus and is approved.

    (iii) **After Effective Date:** Actual sales and deliveries of securities may only be made **after** the effective date, by use of interstate facilities and the U.S. mail (Securities Act §5(a)).

The prospectus must either accompany or precede the delivery of any security (Securities Act §5(b)(2)).

Integrated Disclosure: Corporations subject to the reporting requirements of the Securities Exchange Act of 1934 (The "1934 Act") may incorporate by reference to their 1934 Act filings in their securities registration statements.

Shelf Registration: permits corporations to sell securities, previously registered, *off the shelf* when market conditions are more favorable.
Corporations may offer these securities over a two year period after the effective date of a registration statement by referencing subsequently filed 1934 Act reports (*see* Securities Act Rule 415).

c.   **Relevant Terms explained**:

1.   **Security**: Securities Act §2(1).
(a) Stock, bonds, most promissory notes;
(b) An investment contract or certificate of interest for participation in any profit sharing agreement, regardless of form.

2.   **Offer to sell**: Every attempt or offer to dispose of, or solicitation of an offer to buy, a security or interest in a security, for value (Securities Act §2(3)).

3.   *Any and all activities* designed to stir public interest in a security.
   • **Test:** is whether the activity involves an investment of money in a common enterprise with profits to come solely from the efforts of the other (*See, SEC v. W.J.Howley Co.,* 328 U.S. 29 (1946)).

4. **Sale of Business:** The sale of stock in a business is an ownership transfer. The stock has all the ordinary characteristics of a security.

5. **Promissory Notes: Some promissory** notes are not subject to the Securities Act of 1933.

   A four factor test determines if the note is a security instrument *(Reves v. Ernst & Young, 494 U.S. 56 (1990))*:
   (i) The purchasers or other reasonable persons conceive of it as an investment;
   (ii) The notes are commonly traded as investments;
   (iii) The notes are not subject to some other federal regulation; and
   (iv) The notes bear a strong family resemblance to a non-investment type of financing.

6. **Registration Statement: (Securities Act §7)**
   • A detailed statement of all matters pertaining to the proposed issuance;
   • The form discloses all factors that may effect the fairness of the issue and details the financial status of the corporation;
   • Full details as to the issuer's property and business;
   • The identity and background of all Corporate Officers and Directors;
   • Officers and Directors compensation;
   • The nature of the security being offered: sales, costs, etc.;
   • The underwriting commission and all other related information.

7. **Statutory Prospectus: (Securities Act §10)**
A document filed with the Registration Statement to provide key information contained in the Registration statement.
   - A copy of the prospectus *must* be given to every buyer of securities.
   - If the SEC requires additional information, the corporation must amend the registration statement as requested. The filing of the amendments starts the 20 day period again (*Effective Date*), unless the SEC will agree to an effective date. *See* **Securities Act §8.**

8. **Exempt Securities:** Several types of securities are exempt from the Securities Act's registration requirements but are **not** exempt from the Securities Act's antifraud rules. *See* **Securities Act §3(a).** This includes:
   1. Short term commercial paper;
   2. Securities issued by governmental bodies or charitable institutions;
   3. Securities subject to other government regulation (bank securities and insurance policies).

9. **Exempt Transactions:** Several types of transactions are exempt from the registration requirements of the Securities Act, but the antifraud rules *may* still apply to the following:

   (a) **Ordinary Trading Transactions (Casual Sales Exemption):** The Securities Act exempts transactions by any person other than an issuer, underwriter, or dealer (Securities Act §4(1)).

Exemptions include:

- Ordinary trading transactions between individual investors in securities that *have already been issued.*
- Issuers connected with transactions and others involved with the *initial distribution* of the securities are *not exempt.*

(b) **Exemptions Not Applicable:**

   (i) **Not Applicable to Secondary Distributions** (Securities Act §2(11)).
The exemption does not cover public offerings by a person who acquired the shares from a private placement issuer if the shares were taken with a view to public distribution.
This person is considered an underwriter regardless if otherwise not engaged in the securities business.

   (ii) **Not Applicable to Sales by Control Persons:** The exemption does not cover public offerings by persons who have a control relationship with the issuer. Control persons may be considered the issuer under the Securities Act, and those who distribute the securities for them are underwriters.

        (iii)   **Dealer Sales: (Securities Act §4(3)).**
                Transactions by a dealer (securities broker) **are exempt,** *except*:
                1. During the initial distribution of the securities;
                2. When the dealer is acting as an underwriter of the securities.

10.   **Private Placements: (Securities Act §4(2)).**
Transaction issue not involving any public offering is exempt from registration. Such as:

- An offering to a small number of private subscribers who are sufficiently experienced or informed that the disclosure requirements are not necessary for their protection;
- The private subscribers are acquiring the shares as an investment rather than for public resale.*(SEC v. Ralston-Purina Co., 346 U.S. 119 (1953)).*

Requirement of Available Information:
In addition to being informed and experienced the private subscriber *must have either*:
1. Full disclosure of all the information
2. Have access to such information through an employment or family relationship or by economic bargaining power. *Doran v. Petroleum Management Corp., 545 F.2d 893 (5th Cir. 1977).*

11.   **Small Offerings Under Regulation D:**
During any 12 month period, an issuer may without providing any information, (1) Sell securities up to $1 million to any number of purchasers (Securities Act Rule 504); *OR* (2) Sell securities up to

$5 million to accredited investors (Securities Act §4(6)), which include financial institutions, business development companies, large charitable or educational institutions, the issuer's directors and executive officers, and certain defined wealthy individuals (Securities Act Rule 501, 505). *In addition,* the issuer may add up to 35 ordinary purchasers by providing full disclosure of all information that would have been included in a registration statement to all purchasers.

12. **Investment Intent**:

Stock purchased in a Private Placement offering under Rule 506 or Regulation D can not be offered for resale or distribution to the public.

Purchasers of this type of stock are generally required to sign a letter of investment intent not to offer the stock for resale or distribution to the public. Shares of this sort issued pursuant to this exemption are commonly known as *legended stock or restricted securities.*

13. **Legal Imprint:** Is a notice on the face of the share certificate that the shares have been issued pursuant to an exemption from registration, and may not be freely traded until registered, or further exemption established. The legal imprint under **Rule 144** creates an exemption for resale of such shares (and shares owned by control persons) if, among other things, the following requirements are met:

1. **Public Information:** Specified current public information concerning the issuer.
2. **Holding Period:** No resales of restricted securities are allowed within the first year following issuance.

B.   Rule 10B-5

Introduction
The Securities Act of 1933 (Securities Act);
(1) imposes liability for fraudulent issuance of stock;
(2) prohibits fraudulent sales of securities; and
(3) requires disclosure by public securities issuers.

The Securities Exchange Act of 1934 (Exchange Act):
Mandates the requirements for disclosure, including 10b-5.
Section 10(b)-5 allows for the registration of purchases of
securities.

1.   Rule 10b-5
   a)   Rule 10b-5 prohibits any person, in connection with a
        purchase or sale of any security:
        • To employ any device, scheme, or artifice to defraud;
        • To make any untrue statement of a material fact
          necessary in order to make the statements made, in
          light of the circumstances under which they were
          made, not misleading; or;
        • To engage in any act, practice, or course of business
          which operates or would operate as a fraud or deceit
          upon any person.

   b)   Note that 10b-5 protects purchasing investors and selling
        shareholders. Furthermore, 10b-5 applies to <u>any</u> securities
        transaction and to any fraud in connection with a securities
        transaction, including annual reports, press releases, or any
        other act which may reasonably influence the investing
        public.

   c)   Who may sue under 10b-5:
        Purchasers; and Sellers.
        Exception: all shareholders may sue for injunctive relief
        only *(See Blue Chip Stamps v. Manor Drug Stores)*.

d) Enforcement
  - The SEC can sue to enjoin ongoing violations of Rule 10b-5.
  - Rule 10b-5 also has an implicit private cause of action.

e) Rule 10b-5 Elements:
    1. Material misinformation
    2. Scienter
    3. Reliance
    4. Causation

   (i) **Material misinformation**
     - Prohibits "false or misleading" statements and half-truths. Rule 10b-5 also prohibits a false impression that affects the stock market price of the company.

     - If there is duty to disclose then *silence* violates Rule 10b-5.

     - The Supreme Court has held that materiality exists when a *reasonable investor* would consider the information when evaluating the total circumstances of whether to buy or sell. *Basic, Inc. v. Levinson, supra* (485 U.S. 224 (1988)). The Court held that a corporation must disclose information that is "certain and clear". However, if the information is speculative then disclosure is not necessary. But, if the corporation decides to disclose, the disclosure must be truthful.

(ii) **Scienter**
- A plaintiff, whether it is the SEC or a private plaintiff, must show the defendants scienter to have knowingly embraced the intent to deceive, manipulate, or defraud. *Earnst & Earnst v. Hochfelder*, 425 U.S. 185 (1976).

(iii) **Reliance**
- *Nondisclosure*- If an undisclosed fact is material then there is no need to prove reliance, reliance is presumed.
- *Fraud on the Market*- This leads to a rebuttable presumption of reliance to keep the integrity of stock market prices intact. The stock market prices reflect all known information about the company and when there is false or misleading information it casts doubt on the integrity of market trading.
- *Face-to-Face misrepresentation*- Reliance must be shown in this type of transaction. The plaintiff must show that defendant was aware of the misrepresentation, and that the misrepresentation is material, although plaintiff need not show that he relied on it. This is called the **"reasonable reliance test"**.

(iv) **Causation**
- There are two types of causation that must be shown before a corporation can be held liable:
  1. *Transactional causation*- plaintiff must show "but for" the defendants misrepresentation, plaintiff would not have doubt. *See also* reliance, *supra*.
  2. *Proximate cause*- plaintiff must show that the misrepresentation led to a loss by the plaintiff.

C.   10b-5 and Remedies

1.   Rescission

- *Face-to-face transactions*- plaintiff's sold stock is returned or plaintiff can return the stock for the purchase price.
- *Disgorgement damage*- if the stock was resold, the defrauded seller recovers the buyer's profits (price bought - price sold by defendant). The defrauded buyer recovers his losses (price bought - price resold by plaintiff).
- *Cover damages*- Restores the plaintiff to the position he was in before entering into the transaction.
- All damages are limited to actual damages under the Exchange Act. NO punitive damages may be awarded. A state fraud claim may allow for punitive damages. Check with individual state laws

2.   PSLRA (The Private Securities Litigation Reform Act of 1995)

Changed the pleading requirement for 10b-5 suits. Heightened the pleading requirement, but courts divided as to the exact standard. There are three lines of cases: *See In re Basea Securities Litig. v. Buenos Aires Embotelladora,* 969 F. Supp. 238 (s. D.N.Y. 1997*); In re Silicon Graphics, Inc. Securities Litig.,* 1996 WL 664639 (N.D. Cal. 1996); 311 (N.D.N.Y. 1997); *Pilarczyk v. Morrison Knudson Corp.,* 965 F. Supp. WL 55245 (3d Cir. 1998) (holding that a law firm that was not a signatory to registration materials could be sued in a 10b-5 action).

3. **Insider trading**

a. Definition: The buying or selling of stock with non-public information.

b. Two types of insider trading:
   - *Classic Insider Trading-* where a corporate insider deals in their own company's stock on the basis of non-public information obtained in their corporate capacity; or
   - *Outsider Trading-* where an insider (to a corporation) in his corporate capacity discovers non-public information regarding another corporation and deals in that corporation's stock.

c. Individuals who may be involved in Insider Trading:
   - *Insiders-* People who obtain information because of their corporate position, such as directors, officers, and major stockholders. also known as a Tipper.
   - *Constructive Insider-* People who are affiliated with the corporation such as lawyers, accountant, and investment advisor. Also known as a Tipper.
   - *Tippees-* Persons to whom the insider or constructive insider "tips" (gives) the information to.
   - *Subtippie-* People who are given the information by the tippee of an insider.
   - *Stranger-* People who have no relation to the insider or the corporation but overheard the inside information.

d. Insiders have a fiduciary duty to either disclose non-public information or to abstain from dealing in the stock. *Chiarella v. U.S.*, 445 U.S. 222 (1980).

e. Who has the duty?
   - Insiders- have a duty to disclose or abstain.
   - Tippers- if a tipper knows the information is confidential, the tipper has the duty to disclose or abstain. A tipper can

still be liable even if information is not acted upon if he relays information to the tippee and the information is acted upon.
- Non-insider tippees/subtippees- same as tippee. *see (Dirks v. SEC and Carpenter v. U.S,* 463 U.S. 646 (1983).)
- Stranger- no duty to disclose or abstain as long as no fiduciary relationship to the corporation.

f. Remedies for Insider Trading
- Injunction;
- Disgorgement;
- Civil liability to contempt traders-need and limited to actual profits and losses;
- Civil liability to defrauded parties- can bring 10b-5 action only if they were actually buyers or seller or securities;
- Civil penalties- up to three times the profits realized. An insider or tippee may also be civilly liable to continual traders and defrauded parties;
- Criminal sanctions.

D.   Rule 16b: Short Swing Profits

1.   Purpose

If a director, officer, or 10% beneficial owner sells or buys securities within 6 months of purchase or sale, he is automatically required to_*return "profits" to the corporation, even if they had no insider knowledge.*

Elements:
- Stock listed on national stock exchange; or
- Minimum assets of $5,000,000 and 500 shareholders.

- Person given an honorary title is not liable if they do not perform the duties of that title. Vice versa, a person who does not have a title or is labeled as a lower position can still be liable as a director/officer if they perform the duties.

- Shareholder may sue (even one who didn't own any shares when insider transaction took place).

- Any recovery goes to corporation's treasury, not to the plaintiff-shareholder.

- However, court awards attorney fees to plaintiff's attorneys if the action is successful. These suits are also known as attorney suits.

2.   Public Filings- any purchase/sale which might be a short swing profit must be reported to the SEC under Section 16a.

- Any officer/director/10% beneficial owner must file a statement showing their ownership in the corporation's stock within 10 days after any calendar month in which that ownership changes. The SEC releases this information to the public.

- A Section 16b action must be brought in Federal Court.

  - If the person is a director or officer at the time of either the sale or purchase of stock 16b applies to them. Even if they are not a director or officer at the other end of the transaction 16b also applies to them.

  - Sale, that puts the beneficial owner below 10% - 16b applies:

    Rationale- at the moment director/officer decides to make the sale, he is still more than 10% owner and presumably has access to inside information about the corporation.

    Result- 2 sales: if director/officer is clever, he makes 2 sales to dispose of his interest. If he owns 13%, sells 3.5%, then 9.5%. The director/officer should then argue that he is not liable on the second sale since the 3.5% dropped him below the 10% status. The courts agreed. *(See Reliance Electric v. Emerson)*.

3. Sales Under 16b

- Cash for stock
  Exception- if a corporate raider who owns more than 10%, after realizing that a merger won't occur, tries to find a cash buyer in the market, this may be deemed "voluntary" and, therefore, the raider will be liable under 16b as an unorthodox transaction.
  Merger - 2 Part Test: will be a sale for 16b purposes if the following occur:
  - That the transaction which requires the raider to dispose of his shares was involuntary; and
  - The type of transaction was one which the raider certainly did not have access to inside information.

4. **Computation of Profits under 16b -** Maximum Possible
Profits
- Lowest purchase price matched against highest sale price, and
ignore any loss produced by this method.
- Defendant may have to return "profits" even if he suffered an
overall loss on his short-swing transaction.

TABLE OF CASES

INDEX

A

B

N

O

P